Absentee and Early Voting

Absentee and Early Voting
Trends, Promises, and Perils

John C. Fortier

The AEI Press

Publisher for the American Enterprise Institute

WASHINGTON, D.C.

2006

Distributed to the Trade by National Book Network, 15200 NBN Way, Blue Ridge Summit, PA 17214. To order call toll free 1-800-462-6420 or 1-717-794-3800. For all other inquiries please contact the AEI Press, 1150 Seventeenth Street, N.W., Washington, D.C. 20036 or call 1-800-862-5801.

Library of Congress Cataloging-in-Publication Data
Fortier, John C.
   Absentee and early voting : trends, promises, and perils / by John C. Fortier.
      p. cm.
   Includes index.
      ISBN-13: 978-0-8447-4247-2
      ISBN-10: 0-8447-4247-3
      1. Absentee voting—United States. 2. Voting—United States.
   I. Title

   JK1873.F67 2006
   324.6'5—dc22
                                                            2006024261

11 10 09 08 07 06   1 2 3 4 5 6

Contents

List of Illustrations

Introduction

The United States is in the midst of a revolution in voting. Without great fanfare, our nation is steadily moving away from voting on election day.

Twenty-five years ago, 95 percent of Americans who voted for president cast their votes on the first Tuesday after the first Monday in November. Today, it is fair to say that there are many election days, beginning in September and only culminating on the traditional November date.

The growth of pre–election-day voting is stunning, the variety from state to state enormous, and the implications profound. To put the growth in stark relief, consider that in 1980 approximately four million ballots were cast before election day, compared to over twenty-seven million in 2004. Where one in twenty cast an absentee ballot in presidential elections prior to 1980, today nearly one in four uses one of the several alternatives to election-day polling places.[1]

With the growth in voting before election day came variety among the states. Prior to 1980, all states offered absentee ballots, and a relatively small group of citizens used them, primarily business travelers, senior citizens, the ill and incapacitated, college students, and military and other overseas personnel. While there was some small variation among states in the percentage of absentee votes cast and the rules for casting them, in the core matters there was uniformity. But in the past twenty-five years, not only has the amount of voting before election day skyrocketed, but a variety of methods has proliferated, and the extent of preelection voting now varies widely from state to state. Consider New York, Oregon,

Washington, Texas, and New Mexico. New York in 2004 looked very much like most states did in 1980, with 4.5 percent of voters casting absentee ballots. Oregon, on the other hand, has essentially eliminated the polling place. It employs a vote-by-mail system, where all voters are mailed ballots that they fill out and return to government. In Washington State, almost 70 percent of voters cast absentee ballots. In Texas, there was less than 4 percent absentee voting, but nearly 50 percent of voters voted before election day at an early-voting polling place. In New Mexico, just over 50 percent of voters voted before election day, but 20 percent voted absentee and 30 percent voted at an early-voting location.[2]

Such a dramatic change in our voting patterns is bound to have profound implications, but Americans have resisted reflecting on them. This resistance is understandable for several reasons. The changes have crept up on us quickly. Often, citizens of one state are not aware of dramatic differences in other states and regions. And many of the changes that have brought us where we are have been incremental rather than the products of comprehensive reform.

But real questions should be raised about our move to high rates of pre–election-day voting. Does it raise voter turnout? Does it make voting more convenient? Do voters like the new methods? And, on the more skeptical side, does widespread absentee voting encourage fraud and undermine the secrecy of the ballot? Should third parties, such as the political parties or advocacy groups, be involved in soliciting or collecting absentee ballots? With respect to both absentee voting and early voting at a polling place, are we losing our sense of a civic day of voting? And are voters casting their ballots before critical campaign information is imparted to them?

This study attempts to shed light on where we are, how we got here, what these great changes in our voting before election day mean, and, finally, where we should go in the future.

Chapter 1 is a brief history of absentee and early voting. America first used absentee ballots in a significant way for soldiers during the Civil War. It was not until the early twentieth century that civilian absentee balloting was introduced by the states, although the practice spread quickly to most. A look at the initial adoption of absentee-voting laws is instructive because it highlights the reasons for absentee voting and some of its pitfalls. In brief, reformers who championed absentee voting did so to enfranchise voters in an increasingly mobile society. Troops, railroad workers, the sick, and the elderly were often unable to present themselves at their local election-day polling sites, and thus were unable to vote.

But reformers were also cognizant of the dangers of absentee voting. The late nineteenth century had seen another set of reforms to secure privacy at the voting booth, the so-called "Australian ballot." Reformers wanted to grant access to the ballot for certain classes of voters, but they did not want to wipe away the earlier reforms that had improved the polling place by guaranteeing a secret ballot and reducing fraud. So absentee voting was instituted, but with a series of procedures designed to recreate the privacy of the voting booth as much as possible. This initial tension between access and integrity is an important theme that runs through the history of election reforms, but it is particularly pertinent to recent changes that have spawned significant voting away from the polling place.

The history then recounts the changes in laws and practices from the early part of the twentieth century through the 1970s, including the broadening of the allowable circumstances for absentee voting and its application to specific situations, such as overseas wars. Finally, the chapter recounts the many changes in law and practice of the past twenty-five years, including the introduction of such practices as no-excuses absentee voting, voting by mail, "permanent absentee" status, and early polling-place voting.

Chapter 2 is the most substantial undertaking of this study and the most needed. It assesses the prevalence of absentee and early voting, both at national and state levels, and chronicles the growth in the rates of absentee and early voting over the past twenty-five years. It then categorizes absentee states into four groups: low absentee, high absentee, high early voting, and a mix of absentee and early voting. Getting an accurate picture of absentee and early voting is a very difficult task, especially given the great variety of state and local election and reporting practices, and it involves a great deal of digging and many types of data.

The picture is much more complete because of a survey of the 2004 election conducted by the newly created Election Assistance Commission (EAC) and released in late 2005. As part of this survey of state and local election officials, the EAC was able to collect information on the number of votes cast at election-day polling places, by absentee ballot, at early-polling locations, and by provisional ballot. While successful in collecting data for each state, even this comprehensive survey ran into several problems. Jurisdictions within a number of states failed to report data; data were double-counted; and definitions of the difference between early and absentee voting were inconsistent across the states. The purpose of much of the work of this monograph was to improve upon the data provided by the EAC survey by contacting the states directly for missing or misreported data and recategorizing reported early and absentee votes to reflect the voter experience more accurately. The data collected from state election officials were also supplemented by public opinion survey data. In addition to the 2004 election information, I was able to obtain historical data on absentee and early voting from a number of states, which I used to document the rise in absentee and early voting. Finally, the chapter discusses how the trend toward absentee and early voting is likely to continue, and how early voting is growing at an even faster rate than absentee voting.

Chapter 3 turns to the potential benefits of absentee and early voting, looking in particular at the claim that these practices increase voter turnout, or at least voter convenience. A review of the academic literature finds limited support for the claim that absentee and early voting increases turnout. With the exception of very low-turnout elections, such as local referenda or candidate elections, the increases in turnout are very small at best. Further review shows that any increases in turnout come not from the appeal of early and absentee voting to new voters, but from a somewhat better retention of occasional voters. Finally, the literature shows how mobilization efforts by political parties intersect with these and other new voting methods.

The second part of chapter 3 considers the convenience of absentee and early voting, irrespective of their effects on voter turnout. For election reformers, improving voter convenience may not seem as important as increasing turnout, but it is a good, even if one of the second order. Survey data shed light on voters' desire for convenience and their opinions of absentee and early voting, as well as on inconvenience as a reason for not voting.

Moving away from the potential benefits of voting before election day, chapter 4 examines its potential drawbacks. In particular, it looks at the problems created by the separation of absentee ballots from the polling place and its protections against fraud and coercion. Examples of fraud in recent elections illustrate threats to the integrity of absentee ballots. Also discussed is the troubling role of third parties in the absentee-voting process, and the disadvantage all early voters incur when they miss out on the whole of the campaign and the important communal civic event of a single election day.

Finally, my conclusion digests the trends and the advantages and disadvantages of absentee and early voting and makes recommendations for the future. Current trends toward absentee and early voting, their popularity, and their contribution to voter convenience make it very unlikely that we will ever return to elections in which nearly everyone votes on a single day, no matter how appealing the image might be. To combat the potential loss of the secret ballot and mitigate the potential for fraud, this study recommends the improvement of election-day polling places and the healthy adoption of a period of early voting at polling places, combined with the promotion of early voting at polling places over voting absentee. Recommendations are also made for the several categories of states, tailored to their widely varying rates of absentee and early voting, by addressing specific problems of low-absentee, high-absentee, high-early, and mixed states.

In 2002, Congress enacted the Help America Vote Act (HAVA), which is shaping a great change in state voting practices, including the buying of new voting machines and the creation of computerized statewide voter registration databases. But most of the provisions of HAVA were designed to improve polling-place voting, not to address the now large universe of Americans who vote before election day. Given the high rate of increase in the number of votes cast before election day, it would be wise for citizens and their state governments to turn their gaze to the revolution under their noses, lest the changes become so dramatic that voting is fundamentally transformed without the great deliberation the process deserves.

1

A History of Absentee and Early Voting

Absentee voting arose in the nineteenth and early twentieth centuries out of the needs of a more mobile populace seeking to exercise its right to vote. It was introduced and expanded by advocates for voting by soldiers in the field, railroad workers laying track far from home, business travelers, the elderly, the sick, and vacationers. But the reformers who favored absentee voting were aware of the tension between the easier access it granted and the security of the ballot that it lessened as voters moved away from the protections of a traditional polling place. From its relatively modest origins, absentee balloting, along with mail voting and early voting, became widespread, and it has increased significantly as a percentage of all votes cast. Ease of access continues to grow, but concerns about security remain.

Absentee Voting in the Civil War

The first significant movement for absentee voting occurred during the Civil War. Large numbers of young men who were eligible to vote served in the armies of both the Union and the Confederacy, and, as the 1864 presidential elections approached, spirited legislative battles erupted in the state legislatures over the question of allowing soldiers stationed away from home to cast votes in their home states. In the Union states, some of the impetus behind these battles was partisan, with Republicans pushing for soldier-voting and Democrats opposing these efforts because the soldier vote was for Lincoln. But these debates also raised serious logistical and good-government issues.

How would the votes be cast, by mail or by giving a proxy to some-one at home? How could it be ensured that votes cast in the field were not coerced by commanders or fellow soldiers? How would the votes be delivered, and how could fraud be avoided?[1]

The flurry of state legislative activity also provoked significant legal disputes. Some absentee-ballot laws were struck down by state supreme courts, as they violated state constitutional requirements that citizens vote in person or in their jurisdictions of residence. In response, a number of states amended their constitutions explicitly to allow for absentee voting.[2]

Eventually, nineteen out of the twenty-five Union states passed some form of absentee voting for soldiers in the field, and an esti-mated 230,000 ballots were cast away from traditional polling places in the 1864 presidential election. While the numbers were significant, there were very few places in which the soldier vote made the difference in the election. And there were some accusa-tions of fraud, the most prominent being the case of inspectors appointed by the Democratic governor of New York who were accused of impersonating officers and fraudulently signing and forging officers' names on ballots.[3]

The Introduction of the Secret Ballot in the Late Nineteenth Century

After the Civil War, state laws allowing absentee voting for soldiers generally lapsed or were repealed. During the Spanish-American War, six states passed soldier-voting laws.[4] But except for these and a few other minor state statutes, the issue of absentee voting was not addressed again in a major way by states from the end of the Civil War until the early part of the twentieth century, when they began to introduce limited absentee voting for civilians.

In this interim period, voting in America was significantly reformed, in ways that would affect how absentee balloting was reintroduced in the twentieth century. In the late nineteenth cen-tury, states began to adopt the so-called Australian ballot, which afforded voters many of the protections of the polling place that we take for granted today. Prior to these reforms, many voters were not guaranteed a secret ballot. The worst abuses of the pre–Australian ballot era were perpetrated by party bosses in large cities. In some cases, parties printed their own ballots for their voters to bring with them to the polls. The ballots could be color-coded, and the process of depositing a ballot in a box was open for all to see. This lack of privacy raised the possibility of bribery in the form, for example, of promises of money or job protection in exchange for the "right" vote, as well as other means of reward and coercion.

The Australian ballot provided four improvements in voting:

- Ballots were standardized and printed at public expense to combat the practice of parties or individuals producing their own ballots.

- The names of all of the legal candidates appeared on the ballots.

- Ballots were only distributed by election officers at the polling place.

- Arrangements such as curtains or private booths provided secrecy for casting the vote.

From 1888 to 1910, almost all states adopted some form of the Australian ballot. Although there was subsequently significant debate about how much fraud and corruption were actually present in the system prior to them, the Australian ballot reforms were viewed as substantial and effective at the time they were made. And, in the period following the reforms, there was a drop-off in the voting participation rate, which many reformers attributed to the reduction of fraudulent and coerced votes.[5]

The Introduction of Civilian Absentee Voting in the Early Twentieth Century

The concern with the privacy of the vote that motivated reformers to introduce the Australian ballot became important in the early twentieth-century debate on how to institute absentee balloting. Many advocates of absentee voting feared that the protections won by the reformers might be lost if people were allowed to vote away from polling places. The result was that the first absentee-balloting laws included provisions to protect, as much as possible, the privacy of the vote.

The early part of the twentieth century saw a reform movement for the absentee ballot not unlike that for the Australian ballot thirty years before. Between 1911 and 1938, spurred by the needs of a mobile populace and the experience of soldiers in World War I, all but a handful of states adopted some form of civilian absentee balloting. States differed widely in their absentee-voting systems, and the eligibility to vote absentee was somewhat limited. Some statutes were limited to railroad workers. Others only allowed voting away from the polling place within the voter's home state. Still others were limited to military voters.[6]

Just as military absentee-voting laws had been challenged during the Civil War, many of the new laws for civilians were challenged in state courts on the grounds that they violated state constitutional provisions requiring the secrecy of the ballot. Often at odds with the Australian ballot reforms of the prior generation, some were struck down, while other approaches were modified, and some state constitutions were amended to accommodate the new laws.[7]

Different forms of absentee voting arose to be consistent with state protections of ballot secrecy. One early method allowed for absentee votes to be cast at a polling place in another location in the voter's state, thus providing for all of the protections of the polling place. Some states moved toward a system of mailed absentee ballots, instituting strict regulations to preserve secrecy as much as possible away from the polling place. These often involved procedures by which a voter would have to go to a notary public, show a blank ballot, and then fill out the ballot and seal it, so that the notary public could swear that no one had coerced the person's vote or filled out the ballot on the person's behalf.

Late in the period when this legislation was initially introduced, political scientist Paul Steinbicker noted with approval several provisions that most states had adopted to ensure the integrity of absentee ballots. "The absentee ballot," he wrote,

> is nearly always accompanied by an affidavit blank, usually on the envelope in which the ballot is to be sealed, which must be filled out and attested before a notary or other official authorized to administer oaths [and the] voter shall mark his ballot in the presence of an attesting official, although in such a manner that the latter cannot know for whom or for what it is marked. Usually the attesting official must himself make a jurat to the effect that this has been done.[8]

After the adoption of the first, somewhat limited laws, states began to broaden the eligibility for civilian absentee voting, extending it to the sick, business travelers, and people who could provide valid reasons for being out of state.[9] George Frederick Miller reports, for example, that by 1948, twenty-seven states had absentee-voting laws for the sick.[10]

Absentee Balloting from World War II to the 1960s

During World War II, laws were enacted to promote overseas military voting. Federal law experimented with a federal ballot for overseas soldiers, overrode state poll-tax requirements, and promoted simpler registration and longer lead times for these voters to request, receive, and cast their ballots. These changes early in the war led to only a relatively small amount of overseas military absentee voting in the 1942 elections. Leading up to the 1944 presidential election, however, additional federal legislation was passed, and very significant adoption of overseas military voting laws by state legislatures took place as well. Over two and a half million military voters (not all overseas) cast ballots in 1944, and almost all cast their states' ballots, not federal ballots.[11]

After World War II, many states' overseas military absentee laws expired or were repealed. But with the onset of the Korean War, states again passed such laws, this time of a more permanent character.[12]

The Federal Voting Assistance Act, enacted by Congress in 1955, further eased the process of absentee military voting overseas and included eligible spouses and family members of service personnel. This was eventually broadened to include other nonmilitary voters overseas.[13]

Some limited form of civilian absentee voting had been adopted by almost all the states before World War II. In the late 1950s and '60s, the few that had not provided for it previously did so now. Pennsylvania, for example, introduced civilian absentee voting only after it amended its constitution in the late 1950s, and adopted implementing legislation in the early 1960s.[14]

The 1960s and early 1970s saw further changes in law that broadened the use of absentee voting. Prior to the 1960s, states had significant requirements specifying how long voters must be residents before becoming eligible to register. As of 1960, Alabama, Mississippi, and South Carolina required a two-year residency. Thirty-five states had one-year requirements, and only twelve allowed voting after six months' residency.[15] More than half the states also had local residency requirements, some of them up to a year, which affected people who moved within their states.[16] As the population became increasingly mobile, these requirements had the effect of preventing many Americans from voting, at least for some period of time until residency requirements were satisfied.

This situation began to change in the early 1960s, with recommendations by the National Conference of Commissioners on State Laws. Many states shortened their residency requirements, and they made provisions for people who did not qualify to vote in their states to vote by absentee ballot in their former states. Later, this principle was enshrined in the Voting Rights Act of 1970, which required special registration for presidential elections for new residents of states within thirty days of the election, and the provision of absentee ballots for voting in their former states if they did not meet the requirement.[17]

Along with questions over residency requirements, the reduction of the voting age from twenty-one to eighteen also encouraged absentee voting. The ratification of the Twenty-sixth Amendment made most college students eligible to vote, including many who attended college away from their homes. With many states specifically prohibiting students from registering at their college addresses and the questions surrounding residency requirements just being resolved, the easiest course for many students was to vote absentee.[18]

Absentee Balloting in the 1970s and Early 1980s

In 1975, Congress enacted the Overseas Citizens Voting Rights Act, which allowed overseas voters without legal domiciles in the United States to vote absentee.[19] Overseas absentee voting was further encouraged in 1986 with the enactment of the Uniformed and Overseas Citizens Voting Act, which eased registration requirements and allowed the use of write-in ballots for general federal elections. Under this law, the Federal Voting Assistance Program was created in the Department of Defense to assist overseas voters.[20]

The Move toward "No-Excuses" and Convenience Absentee Balloting

In 1978 California adopted a "no-excuses" absentee-ballot law, which permitted any registered voter to vote absentee. The law repealed the requirement that voters show or claim that they were sick, out of town, or otherwise unable to come to the polling place in order to use an absentee ballot. The absentee-voting rate in California has risen each presidential-year election since this change.[21] In the 1980s and 1990s, many other states adopted this practice, and during the 2004 election, twenty-six states offered "no-excuses" absentee voting. In the 1970s and '80s, many states also began to drop rules requiring witnesses and the use of a notary public to ensure that an absentee ballot had been cast in private without coercion or help from another. By the end of 1991, only eight states required a notary public.[22]

These changes in law and in attitude resulted in an immediate rise in the percentage of absentee voters. The West Coast led the way, with California moving from around 5 percent absentee voting in the late 1970s to over 30 percent in 2004, Washington State moving from 12 percent in 1980 to nearly 70 percent in 2004, and Oregon increasing its absentee voting until it moved to a vote-by-mail system that is essentially 100 percent absentee. Other western states, such as Arizona, Colorado, Hawaii, Nevada, and New Mexico, also increased their absentee voting in the 1980s and '90s, as did several nonwestern states, including Iowa and Vermont.[23]

Oregon's Introduction of Vote by Mail

In the 1980s and '90s, Oregon introduced and began frequently to use a vote-by-mail form of elections. In these elections, ballots are mailed to all voters, who fill them out and return them to government, either by mail or by dropping them off in person. Voters do not have to request ballots or show up at polling places. Other states had previously experimented with vote by mail in very specific circumstances, such as local elections or referenda, or for limited rural precincts where setting up polling places would have been difficult.[24] California held small, special-district elections by mail in the 1970s.[25]

But Oregon would soon be the leader in this practice. In 1980, the Oregon legislature approved a test of the vote-by-mail system in certain local elections, and in 1983 expanded its use to candidate races for office, where it had previously used mail voting only for initiatives. In 1993, the state held its first statewide vote-by-mail election, and in 1998, in a statewide referendum, its citizens voted to use the vote-by-mail system in all future elections.[26]

Permanent Absentee Ballot Status

One other significant development in absentee voting has been the adoption by some states of a designation of permanent absentee status for voters. Voters may indicate that they wish to be sent absentee ballots for all elections until further notice instead of having to request one for each election. By 1998, Oregon, before it switched to all-mail voting, boasted that 41 percent of its registered voters had opted for permanent absentee-voter status.[27]

In the early 1990s, Washington State allowed all voters to apply for permanent absentee status, where it had only been available previously to the sick and the elderly.[28] In 2002, California joined in, and, as of 2005, there were more than 3.3 million permanent absentee voters, or 21 percent of registered voters, in the state.[29]

Early Voting

Like absentee and mail voting, early voting allows a citizen to cast his or her vote prior to election day, but, unlike them, it occurs at a polling place. The forms of early voting and its regulation vary widely from state to state. These include the use of vote centers, which serve a larger area than a precinct; widespread early voting in convenient locations; and voting at county clerks' offices. In many states, the practices of early and absentee voting are intertwined so that it is difficult to distinguish one from the other. In some, a voter showing up at the county government seat to request an absentee ballot might be given the option to vote early onsite. In some, the recording of absentee and early votes is combined.

Many states have had some small amount of early voting for a long time, typically allowing the casting of "absentee" votes in a county clerk's office shortly before election day; but in the 1990s, several states moved to adopt early voting in a significant way. Texas, which began to use early voting in selected elections and counties in the late 1980s, expanded its use in the 1990s. Oklahoma adopted early voting in 1991 and Tennessee, New Mexico, and Nevada in 1994.[30]

A number of states adopted early voting after the 2000 election and have seen significant use of the practice in subsequent elections. Among them are Arkansas, North Carolina, and West Virginia, which have high rates of early voting and low rates of absentee voting, and Florida, which has high rates of both. Texas and Tennessee have the highest rates of early voting. Along with Nevada, they reported over 40 percent in 2004. Arkansas, New Mexico, and North Carolina reported over 25 percent and Florida and Colorado almost 20 percent.[31] A number of states, including Illinois and Maryland, enacted legislation to allow early voting in 2006.

Conclusion

Absentee voting was introduced to make it possible for certain classes of voters to cast their ballots away from their traditional polling places. Whether intended to accommodate soldiers in the field, railroad workers, or the infirm, absentee ballots were seen as an advance by election reformers.

But while reformers saw the necessity of absentee ballots, they also saw the drawbacks. The Australian ballot reforms had instituted measures at the polling place to protect the secret ballot and minimize fraud, and the absentee ballot threatened to skirt the good that had been accomplished by them. Reformers sought to balance the two goods of integrity of the ballot and access to the ballot by requiring voters to meet specific eligibility criteria for voting absentee and to seek out notaries to recreate the secret-ballot protections of the polling place as much as possible.

After the initiation of absentee voting, states expanded the practice by making more classes of citizens eligible to cast absentee ballots in more elections. By the 1970s, most people with legitimate reasons for being away from the election-day polling place were allowed to cast absentee ballots, although they were typically required to provide their reason or at least indicate they had one, and to seek out notaries and/or witnesses to affirm that their votes had been cast properly and without coercion.

Beginning in the late 1970s, some states began to move toward convenience voting, with absentee ballots considered not just a necessary means for those who could not come to the polling place to cast their votes, but a benefit to be extended to anyone who would choose not to vote on election day. This movement for voter convenience increased absentee-voting rates, and ultimately spawned vote by mail in Oregon and early voting in a number of states.

The shift toward convenience altered the balance that had been established by early reformers between access and integrity. It was seen as a nuisance to have to apply for ballots, provide a reason for voting absentee, or have to find a notary public. Advocates saw the vote as too precious to limit with bureaucratic rules and hoped that convenience voting would increase turnout as well as satisfy the voters' desires to make voting easier.

Today, the United States is a patchwork of different voting systems. Some states have large amounts of absentee and early voting, and others do not. The changes have been dramatic but have largely remained under the radar, as a series of incremental decisions in selected states has driven a larger trend. We are no longer a nation that votes nearly exclusively on election day, and the trend toward more pre–election-day voting shows no signs of stopping.

2

The Extent of Absentee and Early Voting and Past and Future Trends

Determining how much voting is going on outside of the traditional polling place is a notoriously difficult task. Election administration in the United States is decentralized to an extreme. Not only are there different state laws and regulations that encourage different forms of voting, but records are not always kept consistently, or at all, from state to state, or even within states from jurisdiction to jurisdiction. A vote that is counted as absentee in one state might be included in the polling-place results of another. Early and absentee balloting might be merged in recordkeeping. Overseas ballots might not be included with other absentee ballots.

While elections will almost certainly always be marked by federalism, there is some hope that we will eventually have a more consistent and accurate picture of voting as the result of the creation of the Election Assistance Commission and its election survey, which was produced for the first time for the 2004 election. Even this extremely comprehensive survey had significant difficulties getting all of the data it requested from state and local jurisdictions. Nonetheless, it is by far the best work that has been done in the area, and the EAC should be able to encourage the production of even better information for its future surveys.

The great diversity of election and recordkeeping practices, however, necessitates use of a variety of sources to supplement the EAC data. These include results from public opinion polls, analysis of state elections laws and practices, and current and historical election data supplied by the states themselves. The broad compilation of data in this study highlights five important features of the rise of absentee and early voting:

- The 2004 election saw a substantial uptick in the percentage of people voting away from the polling place, with approximately 22 percent of voters casting their votes before election day, up from about 14 percent in the 2000 election.

- Voting away from the traditional polling place has increased substantially from twenty-five years ago, when it comprised approximately 5 percent of the votes cast.

- Changes in voting patterns are regional or, in some cases, state to state, with some states, particularly those in the West, reporting large and increasing percentages of absentee or early voting and others almost none.

- Early voting is used extensively in a small number of states, with Texas, Tennessee, North Carolina, New Mexico, and Nevada counting over 25 percent of their votes as cast early, and Florida nearly 20 percent after having recently adopted the practice.

- There is more absentee than early voting, but while absentee voting has increased steadily in the past twenty-five years, early voting has increased at an even faster rate in the past eight (see figure 2-1 on page 38).

Absentee and Early Voting in the 2004 Election

The Election Assistance Commission survey of the 2004 election found that approximately 22 percent, or nearly 28 million out of 122 million votes, were cast early or absentee and away from the traditional election-day polling place. The most comprehensive of its kind, the EAC survey involved extracting data from states and counties about the types of ballots cast, the machines used, error rates, polling places and workers, access of disabled voters, and much more. It was a massive undertaking, and it has yielded important results.

For describing the amount of absentee and early voting rates in our 2004 election, the EAC survey was indispensable. But given the reporting problems inherent in such a massive undertaking, it was necessary to change and update the survey data to give a fuller state-by-state picture. Primarily, this was done by seeking out new or revised information from the states themselves, but it also required other adjustments to the numbers.

Some changes to the EAC data were reclassifications. This study is particularly focused on how much voting occurs outside of the traditional election-day polling place, how much of that is absentee voting, and how much is early voting. As a general concept, it is easy to distinguish between these two forms of voting. An absentee ballot is typically requested by a voter, mailed to that voter, and then filled out and mailed back to the county clerk. Early voting is voting that occurs at a polling place, but before election day. In reality, the distinction is sometimes harder to make. There are many forms of absentee and early voting that fall into a gray area. What about absentee ballots that are dropped off rather than mailed in? What about people who request absentee ballots at a clerk's office but are given the opportunity to fill out the ballot on the spot or to go to a private booth to fill it out? In addition to these difficult definitional questions, states do not have a consistent method of reporting. Many call their absentee ballot programs "early voting" or "advance voting." And the term "in-person absentee" means many different things in different states.

In this analysis, care was taken to recategorize some of the EAC data to reflect the fundamental difference between the two types of voting. Early voting was defined as voting in a polling place before election day. Absentee voting was casting a ballot without the traditional privacy protection of a polling place. If states did not break down their data between these two forms of voting, it was difficult to do it for them. But talking to secretary of state offices, reading election statutes, and investigating election practices in states indicated that some reclassifications were warranted.

Take, for example, two large and relatively uncontroversial cases, Oregon and Arizona. Oregon has a system of voting by mail by which almost all ballots are mailed to voters and then returned by them. The state classifies most of its voting by mail, however, as in-person, polling-place voting, because this system has replaced the traditional polling place. This study recategorizes all of Oregon's vote as absentee. And while Arizona describes all of its voting outside of the traditional election-day polling place as "early voting," it is essentially absentee voting, with some ballots mailed in by voters and others dropped off. Hence, I have recategorized what Arizona reported to the EAC as "early voting" as absentee voting. In considering these changes, I looked at Census Bureau survey data, which indicate on a state-by-state basis whether voters believe they are casting absentee votes or in-person early votes. In both cases, the survey data confirmed that people believed they were voting absentee, not early.

In addition to broad reclassifications, I made other changes to the EAC data. Some states reported totals of election-day, early, absentee, and provisional votes that did not add up to the total numbers of votes cast. Some of these errors were due to double-counting of several categories. I corrected them where I could, especially when they were consistent at the state level. When anomalies were at the county level, it was not possible to determine how each county might have reported its data.

I also filled in missing data. States such as South Carolina, South Dakota, and Mississippi reported nearly all their votes as having come from an unknown source (not polling-place, absentee, early, or provisional voting), but I was able to get data directly from the secretary of state's office.

Finally, in a few states, I made projections. While I was reluctant to move away from the reported data, there were some holes that I tried to fill in with a combination of information from some jurisdictions, survey data, and other evidence of how voting occurred in the state. One example was Maine, which did not report data about absentee or early voting to the EAC or collect these data on a state level but, rather, kept them in the 517 towns in the state. It was not possible to contact all the towns, and there would have been no assurance that they would keep the data or report them in a consistent way. In this case I relied on Census Bureau survey data, which showed that Maine has a relatively high amount of early voting and a modest amount of absentee voting. Numbers, and general descriptions of the voting process obtained from several large jurisdictions in Maine, confirmed this story. For Maine, then, we took the percentages reported in the Census Bureau survey for early and absentee voting and projected them for the vote total of the state.

In two other states, Kansas and South Dakota, there was a firmly reported total of votes cast before election day, but, for a variety of reasons, I believed that the breakdown of that number between absentee and early voting was not properly reflected. Here I used survey data to project the rough percentages of early and absentee voting in each state, and I confirmed them with calls to the secretary of state's office and to several counties that painted the same broad picture. In Pennsylvania, only about two-thirds of the jurisdictions (which cast about 50 percent of Pennsylvania's votes) reported data to the EAC, and the state did not centrally keep data on absentee and early voting. These jurisdictions reported 4.9 percent of their vote as absentee and none as early. Other evidence, including survey data from the census, pointed to the likelihood that Pennsylvania was a low-absentee state. I obtained the total number of ballots cast from the secretary of state's office and projected the 4.9 percent figure to the whole state.

Finally, I found evidence of a small amount of early voting in clerks' offices going on in many states that does not get reported independently, but is merged either with absentee or election-day polling-place data. It was impossible to count these early votes, but public opinion survey data show that this study's supplemented EAC data were able to document most of the early voting

How Much Absentee and Early Voting Occurred in 2004

Over 123 million votes were cast in the 2004 general election. Of those, nearly 18 million, or 14.5 percent, were cast absentee, and over 9 million, or 7.5 percent, were cast early in person (see table 2-1).

TABLE 2-1
ABSENTEE AND EARLY VOTES CAST IN 2004 GENERAL ELECTION

Total Ballots Counted	Absentee Ballots Counted	Absentee Ballot Percent	Early Voting Ballots Counted	Early Voting Percent
123,440,276	17,938,235	14.5%	9,336,486	7.6%

SOURCE: Author's calculations.

These national vote totals come from numbers that states reported to the EAC, modified for this report. They are remarkably consistent with other survey data collected for 2004:

- In the National Election Study, 22.3 percent of respondents indicated that they had voted early or absentee, up from 15 percent in 2000. Breaking this overall number down into absentee and early voting, we found 15 percent responding that they had voted absentee in 2004, up from 10.2 percent in 2000. Early voting was reported by 7.4 percent, up from 5.2 percent in 2000.[1]

- The National Annenberg Election Survey of 2004 reported that 20 percent of voters responded they had voted before election day, up from 14 percent in the 2000 election.[2]

- The U.S. Census Bureau's *Current Population Survey* found a 2004 rate of voting before election day of 20 percent, up from 14 percent in 2000. These overall numbers broke down into 12.9 percent indicating they had voted by mail and 7.8 percent indicating they had voted before election day in person.[3] The Census Bureau data showed 2000 rates of 9.7 percent absentee voting and 3.4 percent early voting.[4]

Further underscoring the magnitude of the change from 2000 to 2004 were changes in the rates of early and absentee voting in the four states that had the most votes cast away from the traditional polling place: California (nearly 4.3 million in 2004, almost all absentee), Texas (3.9 million, almost all early voting), Florida (2.8 million, about one-half absentee and one-half early), and Washington State (2 million, all absentee). Together these states cast nearly half of all votes outside the traditional polling place in 2004 (13 million of the 27 million). All showed substantial increases in the percentages of votes cast. California reported 24.5 percent in 2000 and 32.6 percent in 2004. Texas increased from 39.0 percent to 51.5 percent. Florida increased from 14.0 percent to 36.2 percent. Washington State increased from 54.2 percent to 68.7 percent (see appendix II).

Four Categories of States

Looking at absentee and early voting rates in the 2004 election, the states break down into four categories: states with very little absentee or early voting; states with significant absentee voting but little or no early voting; states with substantial early voting but small amounts of absentee voting; and states that have significant percentages of both absentee and early voting.

Category 1: States with Little or No Absentee or Early Voting. Twenty-four states and the District of Columbia fall into the category of states with little or no absentee or early voting. States are included in this category if the total of their absentee and early ballots is less than 15 percent of their ballots cast (see table 2-2).

Except for Oklahoma, which reports small amounts of both, every state in this category reports low absentee voting and no early voting. This is not to say there is no early voting at a polling place in any of these states. Some allow citizens to cast "absentee" ballots by showing up at the clerk's office prior to the election and voting in a voting booth. But none has a program encouraging early voting, and by most indications very little takes place. Except for Oklahoma, category 1 states reported no early voting in the EAC survey of 2004,[5] and census data confirm only *de minimis* amounts in many. In eleven of these states, less than 1 percent of respondents indicated they had

TABLE 2-2
CATEGORY 1: STATES WITH LITTLE OR
NO ABSENTEE OR EARLY VOTING, 2004

	Ballots Counted	Absentee Ballots	Percent Absentee	Early Ballots	Percent Early
Alabama	1,883,415	63,266	3.4%	—	—
Connecticut	1,595,013	141,698	8.9%	—	—
Delaware	377,407	18,360	4.9%	—	—
District of Columbia	230,105	9,894	4.3%	—	—
Illinois	5,361,048	191,177	3.6%	—	—
Indiana	2,512,142	260,550	10.4%	—	—
Kentucky	1,816,867	98,661	5.4%	—	—
Louisiana	1,943,106	126,581	6.5%	—	—
Maryland	2,395,127	139,440	5.8%	—	—
Massachusetts	2,927,455	145,493	5.0%	—	—
Minnesota	2,842,912	231,711	8.2%	—	—
Mississippi	1,163,460	60,393	5.2%	—	—
Missouri	2,765,960	204,607	7.4%	—	—
Nebraska	792,910	106,552	13.4%	—	—
New Hampshire	686,390	62,059	9.0%	—	—
New Jersey	3,639,612	194,168	5.3%	—	—
New York	7,448,266	337,544	4.5%	—	—
Ohio	5,730,867	611,210	10.7%	—	—
Oklahoma	1,474,304	64,076	4.3%	85,603	5.8%
Pennsylvania	5,769,590	282,710	4.9%	—	—
Rhode Island	440,743	19,271	4.4%	—	—
South Carolina	1,631,156	157,990	9.7%	—	—
Utah	941,215	57,443	6.1%	—	—
Virginia	3,223,156	221,890	6.9%	—	—
Wisconsin	3,025,801	366,048	12.1%	—	—
Total	62,618,027	4,172,792	6.7%	85,603	0.1%

SOURCE: Author's calculations.

voted early, and, in seventeen, less than 2 percent did.[6] These very small amounts of early voting look very different from the results of the concerted efforts of states in category 3 (see below), where large portions of the electorate are encouraged to vote early.

The states in category 1 look much as most of the country did before 1980, when absentee balloting was used by relatively small classes of people, especially those out of town on business, those too ill or frail to make it to the polls, and those with long-term commitments elsewhere, such as military personnel, college students, and retirees with second homes in other states. Not surprisingly, most of the states that still have restrictions on absentee balloting are in this group. Seventeen do not have no-excuses absentee voting—that is, they require voters to provide a reason for voting absentee.[7]

Several states in category 1 have seen their absentee-voting rates creep up, and they may well find themselves in the high-absentee category before long. Four have rates of over 10 percent. Wisconsin's absentee-ballot rate increased from 4.6 percent in 1996 to 6.1 percent in 2000, and to 12.1 percent in 2004. Nebraska's went from 6 percent in 1996 to 11.5 percent in 2000, and to 13.4 percent in 2004.

But it is interesting to note that a number of states have shown very low and steady rates of absentee voting. Rhode Island, for example, had a rate of 4.5 percent in 1980 and has had a rate between 3.5 and 4.5 percent in each presidential election since.[8] Similarly, New Hampshire reported a rate of 7.8 percent in 1980 and has seen rates between 7 and 9 percent each presidential election since.

In addition to those in category 1, there are several states with low absentee rates listed in other categories. All five heavy early-voting states report rates of absentee voting below 5 percent: Arkansas, North Carolina, Tennessee, Texas, and West Virginia. Idaho (5.6 percent) would also appear on this list but for the fact that it has a moderately high rate of early voting that pushes the total of absentee and early voting over 15 percent, thereby placing it into the mixed category.

There are clear regional differences with respect to how much early and absentee voting occurs. Almost all of the northeastern states are in the low-absentee category. These include four of the six

New England states, plus New York, New Jersey, Pennsylvania, Delaware, Maryland, the District of Columbia, and Virginia. Vermont and Maine are the only northeastern states not on this list. Some midwestern states, such as Ohio, Indiana, Illinois, Minnesota, Missouri, and Kentucky, are low-absentee states, as are a few states in the Deep South: Alabama, Louisiana, South Carolina, and Mississippi. The only western state on the list is Utah.

Overall, this group of low-absentee states is the largest of our four categories, comprising just under half of the states, 48.7 percent of the estimated voting-age population, and 50.9 percent of ballots cast. Yet these states cast only 23.3 percent of absentee ballots. Combined, they showed a 6.7 percent rate of absentee voting, compared to a national rate of 14.5 percent. They also cast less than 1 percent of the nation's in-person early votes.

Even though absentee and early voting have increased signifi- cantly, this very large group of states has not followed that trend. Still, it is likely that some will move out of the category in 2008. For example, Illinois and Maryland have enacted early voting, and if they follow the pattern of other states, they will generate over 15 percent of their votes from early voting alone.

Category 2: High-Absentee States with Little or No Early Voting. Eleven states fall into the second category, with over 15 percent of their votes cast absentee and with less than 5 percent in-person early voting. Except for Michigan, all offer no-excuses absentee ballots.[9] Only three states report any early voting (see table 2-3), although, as in low-absentee states, there may be small amounts occurring at clerks' offices in some of the others.

Among high-absentee states, Oregon and Washington are in a class by themselves. Oregon has held all of its elections by an all- mail ballot since 1998. Washington casts nearly 70 percent of its votes absentee. Another three states, Arizona, California, and Iowa, top 30 percent. The remaining states in this category cluster around 20 percent.

In addition to these, several states in the mixed category feature absentee-ballot rates that would place them in category 2 were it

TABLE 2-3
CATEGORY 2: HIGH-ABSENTEE STATES WITH LITTLE
OR NO EARLY VOTING, 2004

	Ballots Counted	Absentee Ballots	Percent Absentee	Early Ballots	Percent Early
Alaska	314,502	62,017	19.7%	10,894	3.5%
Arizona	2,038,077	830,874	40.8%	—	—
California	12,589,683	4,105,179	32.6%	—	—
Iowa	1,497,741	460,059	30.7%	—	—
Michigan	4,876,237	861,305	17.7%	—	—
Montana	456,096	91,076	20.0%	—	—
North Dakota	316,049	51,116	16.2%	6,523	2.1%
Oregon	1,851,671	1,851,671	100.0%	—	—
Vermont	313,973	60,072	19.1%	—	—
Washington	2,885,001	1,982,457	68.7%	—	—
Wyoming	245,789	47,008	19.1%	230	0.1%
Total	**27,384,819**	**10,402,834**	**38.0%**	**17,647**	**0.1%**

SOURCE: Author's calculations.

not for their significant in-person early voting rates: Colorado (27.9 percent absentee), New Mexico (20.1 percent), Hawaii (19.3 percent), and Florida (17.5 percent).

Of the eleven states in category 2, seven are in the West, and three Great Plains states are represented. Vermont is the only eastern state, and there are none from the South.

Overall, these high-absentee states comprise 23 percent of the U.S. voting-age population, cast 22.3 percent of all ballots, and cast 58.1 percent of the nation's absentee ballots. The three Pacific Coast states, California, Oregon, and Washington, cast over three-quarters of the absentee ballots in this group and over 40 percent of the national total. Combined, the states in this category show a 38 percent rate of absentee voting, compared to 14.5 percent nationally. They cast less than one-quarter of 1 percent of the in-person early votes in the country.

TABLE 2-4
CATEGORY 3: HIGH EARLY-VOTING STATES, 2004

	Ballots Counted	Absentee Ballots	Percent Absentee	Early Ballots	Percent Early
Arkansas	1,025,078	41,432	4.0%	293,084	28.6%
North Carolina	3,571,420	122,984	3.4%	984,298	27.6%
Tennessee	2,458,213	57,676	2.3%	1,102,513	44.9%
Texas	7,507,333	283,159	3.8%	3,580,330	47.7%
West Virginia	769,645	20,004	2.6%	126,503	16.4%
Total	15,331,689	525,255	3.4%	6,086,728	39.7%

SOURCE: Author's calculations.

Category 3: High Early-Voting States. Large-scale, in-person early voting is a relatively new phenomenon, but it has reached significant proportions in a number of states. The five in category 3 have at least 15 percent of their ballots cast in person at early-voting polling places, and they have less than 5 percent absentee voting (see table 2-4). Each has a policy of no-excuses in-person early voting, but they require citizens to give a reason if they wish to vote absentee.[10]

Texas and Tennessee are clearly the leaders in category 3, with nearly 50 percent in-person early voting. They are also the "veterans" in promoting large-scale early voting, having started the practice in the late 1980s and early 1990s, respectively. Arkansas and North Carolina both generate nearly 30 percent early voting, and West Virginia, 16.4 percent. All of these states reached these levels after only a small number of elections.

Several states in the mixed category feature high rates of in-person early voting that would place them in category 3 were it not for their significant absentee voting: Nevada (41.7 percent), New Mexico (30.5 percent), Colorado (19.2 percent), and Florida (18.7 percent).

Regionally, the five states in category 3 form a band of contiguous states, cutting across the South and border states. There are no eastern, western, or midwestern states in the group. Maryland and Illinois, which border these states, enacted early voting for the future.

Category 3 states make up only 13.9 percent of the voting-age population and cast only 12.5 percent of the nation's ballots. However, they make up 65.6 percent of the in-person early ballots cast. Combined, they have an early-voting rate of 39.7 percent. They cast only 2.9 percent of the nation's absentee ballots.

With several states having adopted or considering adopting early voting, this category is likely to grow by 2008.

Category 4: Mix of High-Absentee and Early Voting. Ten states have significant usage of both forms of convenience voting. By definition, this group has at least 15 percent early and absentee voting combined and at least 5 percent of each (see table 2-5).

Viewed as a group, these states have relatively equal amounts of absentee and early balloting, with 15.7 percent absentee and 17.4 percent early. Six of the ten have more early than absentee balloting and four vice versa.

The totals of absentee plus early voting vary greatly among the states. Nevada leads the way with 52.9 percent of its vote cast away from the traditional polling place, third in the nation behind Oregon and Washington. New Mexico also has over 50 percent, and Colorado is not far behind with 47.1 percent. Florida and Hawaii are in the middle of the group with over 30 percent, and the remaining states have between 15 and 25 percent.

Almost all of the category 4 states are in the West. Florida, Georgia, and Maine are the only eastern states on the list, with Florida having moved from being a no-early-voting, low-absentee state in 2000 to having 36.2 percent of its votes cast either early or absentee in 2004. There are no midwestern states on the list.

Overall, the mixed states make up 14.6 percent of the population. They cast 14.6 percent of the votes, 33.7 percent of the early ballots, 15.8 percent of absentee ballots, and 21.9 percent of all votes cast away from traditional election-day polling places.

TABLE 2-5
CATEGORY 4: MIX OF HIGH-ABSENTEE AND EARLY VOTING, 2004

	Ballots Counted	Absentee Ballots	Percent Absentee	Early Ballots	Percent Early
Colorado	2,148,036	600,075	27.9%	412,280	19.2%
Florida	7,639,949	1,336,297	17.5%	1,428,362	18.7%
Georgia	3,317,336	282,857	8.5%	387,596	11.7%
Hawaii	431,203	83,098	19.3%	50,223	11.6%
Idaho	612,786	34,609	5.6%	59,239	9.7%
Kansas	1,199,590	134,361	11.2%	116,353	9.7%
Maine	754,777	80,761	10.7%	50,570	6.7%
Nevada	831,833	93,364	11.2%	346,823	41.7%
New Mexico	775,301	156,020	20.1%	236,340	30.5%
South Dakota	394,930	35,912	9.1%	58,722	14.9%
Total	**18,105,741**	**2,837,354**	**15.7%**	**3,146,508**	**17.4%**

SOURCE: Author's calculations.

When Voters Cast Their Ballots in 2004

The National Election Study (NES) asks its respondents whether they voted on election day or before, and of those who voted before, it asks how far in advance they did so. In 2004, 12.7 percent of voters indicated that they voted one week or less prior to election day, 6.6 percent voted between one and two weeks prior, and 3.1 percent voted more than two weeks prior. The rate of voting in all of these categories was higher than in 2000, when 9.3 percent voted one week or less, 4.5 percent one to two weeks, and 1.5 percent more than two weeks before election day (see table 2-6).

Most early voting occurs in the week before the election. In 1996, about 62 percent of pre-election day voting took place in that week; in 2000 the figure was 61 percent, and in 2004 it was 57 percent. About 14 percent occurred two weeks or more before the election in 2004, up from 10 percent in 2000 and 11 percent in

TABLE 2-6
TIME OF VOTE (BEFORE ELECTION DAY)
AS PERCENTAGE OF WHOLE VOTE, 2004

	1 week or less	1 to 2 weeks	2 or more weeks
1996	7.83%	3.40%	1.45%
2000	9.31%	4.48%	1.52%
2004	12.66%	6.57%	3.11%

SOURCE: See note 27 on page 96.
NOTE: Percentage of respondents who indicated whether they voted either on or before election day. Several categories are combined to make the one week or less and the two or more weeks categories.

1996. Even with an increase in 2004, the rate of voting more than two weeks in advance of election day was small, at only 3.1 percent of the electorate.

One possible reason this last number has risen is an increase in opportunity to vote more than two weeks in advance of the election. Absentee voting and voting by mail allow citizens to cast ballots even earlier than they could in most in-person early-voting locations. To comply with federal law regarding overseas and military voters, ballots must be ready to be sent out forty-five days before an election. Most states allow absentee ballots to be cast well before two weeks prior to the election; Oregon mails ballots out to all voters six weeks prior.

As for the major early-voting states, most designate a period of two to two and a half weeks prior to the election for voting. Georgia has early voting for one week before election day. New Mexico is at the other end of the spectrum: early voting begins there forty days in advance.

The opportunity to vote very early continues to rise, as some states adopt relatively long periods of early voting, and some encourage more absentee voting. There may also be a countertrend, however. Michael W. Traugott and Michael Hamner looked at the time of voting in Oregon's mail-voting system and found that since vote by mail was introduced statewide, the percentage of voters holding their ballots closer to election day has grown steadily.[11] If this turns out to be a more general phenomenon, it may be that as early and absentee voting systems become established, people will vote later than they did when their systems were new. Examining the same data in a different light, Paul Gronke found that early votes are cast closer to election day when there is a hard-fought race, and sooner when there is not.[12]

Finally, as several studies have found that more partisan and informed citizens vote early and absentee, election-day voters are more likely than pre–election-day voters to use campaign information from candidate and other groups to make their decisions.[13] Clearly, more people are voting before the election, and more people are voting two weeks or more before the election. But, given the variety of findings, it is not clear that increased voting more than two weeks before the election represents a trend or a temporary increase concomitant with the introduction of new programs of early and absentee voting.

Substantial Increase in Absentee and Early Voting since 1980

A number of measures show that prior to 1980, absentee voting was a relatively small phenomenon, but it has increased steadily in the past twenty-five years. The best evidence indicates that the rate of absentee voting from the 1940s to 1980 was relatively stable and amounted to between 4 and 5 percent of votes cast in presidential election years. In the 1980s, the rate began to rise, and continued to do so in the 1990s and in each of our recent presidential elections. Approximately 15 percent of all votes in the 2004 election were cast absentee. Early voting has become a significant phenomenon only in the past ten years, expanding from almost none to about 7.5 percent of the vote in that period.

Prior to 1980. There is little solid evidence for national rates of absentee voting prior to 1980. The following information is available for some presidential elections for the period, beginning with the 1860s:

- In the early part of the twentieth century, historian Josiah Benton, who had himself voted in the field as a young soldier in the Civil War, made a series of estimates about the extent of absentee military voting in the 1864 presidential election. By extrapolating data from states that kept accurate records to others that permitted absentee voting, he concluded that 230,000 votes were cast in the field out of 4 million votes cast nationwide. This would constitute 5.8 percent.[14] Such a level would not be reached again for a very long time.

- After the adoption of civilian absentee voting by most states in the early part of the twentieth century, political scientist Paul Steinbicker estimated that 2 percent of the 45 million votes cast in the 1936 election were cast absentee.[15]

- The 1944 election was held when many eligible voters were at war overseas. An American Political Science Association (APSA) report issued in 1952 found that 2.5 million military absentee ballots were cast in 1944.[16] As there were 48 million votes cast in the election that year, the military absentee vote alone amounted to a rate surpassing 5 percent of the total.

- William Andrews estimated that 4.9 percent of votes cast in the 1960 election were by absentee.[17]

- In 1968, the National Election Survey asked voters whether they had voted in person or by absentee ballot. Absentee ballot was indicated by 4.3 percent of respondents.[18]

Although state data are spotty prior to 1980, the early leader in absentee voting, California, has numbers going back to the early 1960s. There, from 1962 to 1976, absentee voting remained stable, at between 4 and 5 percent of the vote, in presidential election years. In 1978, California instituted no-excuses absentee voting, and the rate immediately rose to 6.2 percent. Since then, the percentage has increased with each presidential election.

Several states that have high rates of absentee voting today had much lower rates in 1980. Vermont reported 8 percent absentee voting in 1980, versus 19.1 percent today. Washington State showed 12.2 percent—high for 1980, but modest compared to its subsequent meteoric rise to 68.7 percent in 2004. And states such as New Hampshire and Rhode Island showed low rates of absentee voting that have not changed significantly in the past twenty-five years.[19]

The 1980s—The Beginning of the Rise of Absentee Voting. In the 1980s, absentee voting rates began to rise from the relatively stable 4–5 percent that had prevailed since World War II to the nearly 15 percent level of 2004. This increase was concentrated in specific states, with many others not participating in the trend. In fact, the rise of absentee voting was not a coincidence, but was actively pushed by certain states. During the 1980s some states began to loosen their rules about who could vote absentee, with some adopting no-excuses absentee voting. And some began to do away with requirements for notaries and witnesses to the casting of absentee ballots. Overall, absentee voting rose from approximately 5 percent in 1980 to 7–8 percent in 1992.[20]

The evidence of the growth of absentee voting nationally comes from the Census Bureau survey. In 1980, 4.3 percent of respondents reported voting absentee; that number rose to 5.3 percent in 1984 and 7.5 percent in 1992.

State data confirm this trend. Much of the rise in the national rate of absentee voting can be attributed to California, which instituted no-excuses absentee voting in 1978 and precipitated a steady increase in the state.[21] From the early 1960s to the late 1970s, California reported a stable 4–5 percent of the vote as absentee in presidential elections. This changed with an uptick to 6.2 percent in 1980. In the period from 1980 to 1992, when the national rate of absentee voting rose from 4.3 to 7.5 percent, California increased its rate from 6.2 to 17.2 percent. The California increase alone accounts for over one-third of the national increase in this period; Washington State also saw significant change, starting with a high 12.2 percent rate of absentee voting in 1980 and increasing to 18 percent in 1992.[22]

Other states did not show a change in their absentee rates in the early 1980s. Rates in New Hampshire and Rhode Island were similar to their rates today. Vermont increased from about 8 percent absentee voting in 1980 to 9.3 percent in 1988, but its larger increases occurred in the 1990s.

The 1990s—Continued Growth in Absentee Voting. Absentee voting continued to rise significantly in the 1990s, with the rise again occurring in selected states. National survey data chronicle this trend. The Census Bureau data indicate an increase from 7.4 percent in 1992 to 9.8 percent in 2000. During this period, the Census Bureau changed the question it asked to determine whether voters were voting by absentee or at early-voting polling places before election day. In 1992, respondents were asked about the time of day they had voted on election day, or if they had voted absentee. Starting in 1996, the question was whether they voted before election day and whether they voted absentee or early in person. While it is possible that the pre-1996 surveys caused some respondents who voted early in person to indicate that they voted absentee, it is also the case that 1996 coincides with the wide-scale use of early voting in Tennessee (Texas had already seen significant early voting in 1992). And the small initial response shows that the question was asked at an opportune time, when early voting in person was just beginning to be a real option in some states.[23]

Survey data from the National Election Studies show that the national rate of absentee voting in 1992 had risen higher than our pre-1980 estimate of 4–5 percent. NES respondents indicated nearly 8 percent absentee voting in 1992, and the rate continued to rise through 2000, when it stood at over 10 percent, and 2004, when it rose to 15 percent. The NES, like the Census Bureau, also changed its questions in 1996 to reflect whether people had voted early or absentee.[24]

Survey data from the census and NES together indicate a rise in the national absentee ballot rate from 7.5 to 8 percent in 1992, to 10 percent in 2000. State data from the period again bear out this trend.[25] California moved from 17.2 percent in 1992 to 20.3 percent in 1996, and then to 24.5 percent in 2000 and 32.6 percent in

2004. Washington State went from 18 percent in 1992 to 35.6 percent in 1996, to 54.2 percent in 2000 and 68.7 percent in 2004. Oregon went from 48 percent in 1996 to 100 percent in 2000 and 2004, when it employed all-mail voting. Much of the national growth in the national rate of absentee voting in the 1990s can be attributed to these states. Of course, there is evidence that several other states were also increasing their rates of absentee voting, including Iowa, whose rate was 10.2 percent in 1992, 15.9 percent in 1996, 21.2 percent in 2000, and 30.7 percent in 2004. Vermont went from 9.1 percent in 1992 to 19.2 percent in 2000, and Hawaii from 10.6 percent in 1992 to 19.7 percent in 2000.[26]

Early Voting: The Rise in the 1990s. In 1996, the two national surveys began to distinguish between early and absentee voting. The Census Bureau found that 2.4 percent of voters voted early in person in 1996, rising to 3.9 percent in 2000 and 7.8 percent in 2004. NES found a similar trend, but with somewhat different numbers. In these surveys, early voting comprised 4.6 percent of voting in 1996, 5.2 percent in 2000, and 7.4 percent in 2004.[27]

Statewide data underscore the changes that have taken place in the area of early voting. Texas began early voting in the late 1980s and quickly reached a level of over 20 percent of the vote. By 1992, it had reached 33 percent, which increased to 39 percent in 2000, and further increased to 47.7 percent in 2004. Tennessee instituted early voting in 1994. The state had essentially no early voting in 1992, 21 percent in 1996, 36 percent in 2000, and 44.9 percent in 2004.[28] A rough estimate shows that Texas and Tennessee accounted for nearly all of the national early voting in 1996, about three-quarters in 2000, and just over half in 2004.[29]

As of 2004, Texas and Tennessee are still the leaders in the rates of early voting, and together they cast nearly 50 percent of all early ballots; but there are other large players as well. More early ballots were cast in Florida than in Tennessee in 2004, and North Carolina was not far behind. While the number of states with significant early voting is still relatively small, those that have adopted the practice have reached high percentages very quickly.

FIGURE 2-1
EARLY AND ABSENTEE VOTING, 1980–2004

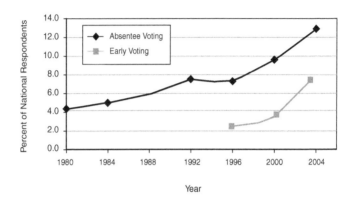

SOURCE: U.S. Census Bureau, "Voting and Registration," *Current Population Surveys 1998–2006*, http://www.census.gov/population/www/socdemo/voting.html (accessed August 15, 2006).

Early Voting Is Growing Even Faster than Absentee Voting. Absentee voting has been on the rise since 1980, with its rate more than tripling since that time. Early voting has more than tripled since 1996 (see figure 2-1).

Beyond the data already cited, one other indication of the quick rise of early voting is how large a percentage of it is recorded when states offer the option in a presidential election for the first time. Tennessee, Florida, West Virginia, Arkansas, and North Carolina all showed rates of at least 15 percent in the first elections in which their residents were allowed to vote early. Moreover, Texas and Tennessee were able substantially to increase their rates of early voting after its initial introduction. Tennessee, for example, had over 40 percent early voting after only three presidential elections.

By contrast, even high-absentee states have, for the most part, seen their rates of absentee voting increase much more incrementally. Only Oregon, in its move to mail voting, and Washington State have shown rates of growth in absentee voting comparable to those in early voting in Texas and Tennessee. More typical have been California, Hawaii, Iowa, North Dakota, and Vermont, where increases in rates of absentee voting have been steady, but have not taken the large jumps registered in early voting in Texas and Tennessee.[30]

Conclusion

Absentee voting and early voting have risen dramatically. Starting in the late 1970s, selected states began to encourage absentee voting, and, since 1980, the practice has increased more than threefold to nearly 15 percent of all votes cast. Early voting was adopted in a substantial way by several states beginning in the 1990s, and early voting rates have gone from essentially 0 to 7.5 percent of all votes cast.

Most pre–election-day votes are cast in the week before election day, with a quarter of early votes coming in from one week to two weeks before the election, and a relatively small share more than two weeks before. But, at least according to one survey, the number of very early voters rose in 2004.

The national trends tell only part of the story, because individual states have taken very different paths. While there is great variety of practice in America, our states fall into four categories: those with low absentee rates (still the largest group); those with high absentee rates; those with high rates of early voting at polling places; and those with high rates of both absentee and early voting.

The trend toward more voting before election day shows no sign of stopping. Absentee voting rates will likely increase again in 2008, and early voting will likely continue its more dramatic rise. Since 2004, several more states have already adopted early voting for future elections.

These changes and prospects for future change represent a revolution in voting. Without a national debate, America has gone in the past twenty-five years from a nation where one in twenty voters casts an absentee ballot to one in which nearly one in four votes before election day.

3

Absentee and Early Voting:
Voter Turnout and Voter Convenience

A number of benefits are ascribed to absentee and early voting. This study will not address the questions of financial cost or of convenience for election administrators. It will, however, address two central claims made about methods of pre-election day voting: that they increase voter turnout, and that they are convenient for voters.

Voter Turnout

The United States has low voter turnout rates compared to other democracies. Many civic-minded reformers believe these rates should be raised by removing obstacles to voting, and proponents of absentee voting, early polling-place voting, and mail voting see these methods as means to accomplishing this. Their motto could be, "Remove the barriers to voting, and they will come."

The greatest promoters of this view are the states which have most fully adopted absentee and mail voting, Oregon and Washington. In 2001, Bill Bradbury and Sam Reed, then secretaries of state of, respectively, Oregon and Washington, published an opinion piece in the *New York Times* touting the benefits of mail and absentee voting. At the heart of their case was the claim that voting by mail increases voter turnout:

> The advantages of voting by mail become clear when
> you look at turnout. When Oregon launched its first

all-mail primary election in 2000, there were 16 percent more votes cast than had been cast in any primary done entirely at polling stations. Last fall, nearly 80 percent of registered voters participated in Oregon's first all vote-by-mail presidential election, as opposed to 51 percent voter turnout nationwide.

Washington's experience, although more limited in scale, has been similar. When the state conducted a referendum on building a new football stadium in Seattle in 1997, 27 of the state's 39 counties conducted the entire election by mail. The results were stunning: for example, in Pacific County, which used polling stations only, 39 percent of registered voters turned out; adjacent Wahkiakum County, which used vote-by-mail, had a 62 percent turnout.

We've also found that vote-by-mail dramatically increases turnout in national elections during the off-Presidential years when voters' interest tends to drop. In 1998, turnout in both Washington and Oregon was roughly 9 percentage points higher than the national average.[1]

These claims about voter turnout did not go unchallenged. Curtis Gans, for one, director of the Center for the Study of the American Electorate, disputed Oregon's claims by noting that 1998 was a peculiar year, with both Senate seats up for election. Gans also put the 2000 Oregon turnout in perspective; it was up, but by less than other battleground states. Finally, he showed that Oregon had been a high-turnout state before its vote-by-mail system, featuring the country's sixth-highest turnout both before and after it adopted mail voting in 1998.[2]

While Oregon and Washington have remained great promoters of mail voting, a growing academic literature paints a much more restrained picture of the effects of absentee and early voting on turnout, more consistent with Gans's criticisms than the claims of Bradbury and Reed.

Voting Absentee and by Mail and Voter Turnout

The academic literature has presented several findings on voter turnout and mail and absentee voting:

- Turnout is positively affected by voting by mail in very low-turnout elections, such as local elections and initiatives. Several early studies on mail voting looked at local elections and initiatives. Before Oregon began to employ a vote-by-mail system in all of its elections, several other states used it for limited purposes. Nearly one thousand elections were held before 1988, many of them local referenda.[3] David Magleby looked at a number of these elections and found that mail voting increased turnout by 19 percent.[4] In another study, Karp and Banducci found support for the same general principle that the most significant increases in turnout in vote-by-mail elections occur in low-turnout elections.[5]

- There is little evidence of a turnout effect on higher-profile elections. At best, studies show a very small turnout effect, derived more from slightly better retention of habitual voters than from attraction of new voters. A number of studies have found that voting by mail did increase turnout by modest amounts. South-well and Burchett found turnout up an average of 10 percent in the Oregon elections they studied, but, as Traugott notes, only 5–7 percent in typical elections.[6] Berinksy, Burns, and Traugott found a 4–6 percent increase in turnout in the 2000 Oregon general election.[7]

   Gans cast doubt on the prospect of even a small positive turnout by noting that in both presidential and midterm elections, states with easy, no-excuses absentee voting had smaller increases in turnout than those with traditional absentee-ballot regimes. Gans attributes the poor performance of absentee voting to the fact that turnout efforts are diffused if spread over a long period of time. Also, his specific criticism of Oregon's vote-by-mail system, quoted earlier, takes a different tack than many of the studies that have focused on increases in turnout within the state. Gans compared Oregon's turnout performance to other states and found that voter turnout did not increase relative to other battleground states.[8]

- Increases in turnout from mail voting come from a greater retention of sometime-voters rather than the attraction of new voters. In their study of Oregon's vote-by-mail elections, Berinsky, Burns, and Traugott observed a modest increase in turnout, but found that it came primarily from higher rates of voting among occasional voters, not from the attraction of nonvoters to the polls. Vote by mail mobilized some "who were predisposed to vote—those individuals who are long term residents and who are registered partisans—to turn out at higher rates than before."[9] Karp and Banducci also found this effect, noting that "these low stimulus elections, when conducted by mail are likely to expand the pool of voters to include those who already participate in high stimulus elections but cannot be bothered to go to the polls in low saliency elections."[10] Berinsky found this phenomenon more generally in all election reforms, from motor-voter registration to vote by mail to early voting. Those who take advantage of these methods are not typically the poor or nonvoters, but are more knowledgeable than average about the election and are prior voters.[11]

- Political party mobilization efforts often work hand-in-hand with mail voting, and small increases in turnout may be attributable to that mobilization. In an early study, Eric Oliver found that liberalized absentee voting did lead to modestly higher turnout, but only when combined with party mobilization. When a party, in this case the Republican Party, tried to mobilize its voters to vote absentee, there was an increase in turnout.

Liberalized absentee laws without such mobilization did not show such an increase.

Specifically, when parties sent out pre-filled absentee ballot applications, recipients were more likely to register as absentee voters and more likely to vote. Oliver took from this that liberalized absentee voting was not in itself easier than absentee voting with restrictions, but a pre-filled ballot application was more convenient.[12]

Several other studies back up this finding. Stein, Leighley, and Owens found that party mobilization increased preelection voting.[13] Patterson and Caldeira saw higher rates of absentee voting in states where a party made an effort to have voters cast absentee ballots.[14] Gronke et al. found that Hispanics in Florida had higher rates of voting before elections than other minority groups because of mobilization efforts of the "Mel Martinez for Senate" campaign.[15]

- As large-scale mail and absentee balloting is relatively new, researchers express concern that small increases in turnout might be attributable to the novelty and promotion of the new voting systems by election officials. Several researchers have qualified their findings of positive turnout effects by noting the newness of the phenomenon they are studying. New methods of voting might attract voters, until the magic wears off. And new methods of voting are often promoted by government more than the old, so it might be the government effort to publicize the method that increases turnout, not the method itself. In 2004, Traugott already saw signs that the novelty of Oregon's vote-by-mail system was wearing off.[16]

As a whole, the academic consensus is that mail and absentee balloting has little or no effect on voter turnout except in low-turnout elections, and that turnout effects may be short-lived, dependent on party mobilization, and not likely to attract new voters to participate.

Early Voting and Turnout

Early voting, like vote-by-mail and absentee voting, holds out the promise of increasing voter turnout. More days in which to vote might lead to more voting. But the academic literature has not shown a consensus that this actually happens.

Robert Stein and Patricia Garcia-Monet were among the first to look at early voting in Texas. They found that while it did raise turnout in Texas in the 1992 presidential election, the effect was quite small. For each 1 percent increase in the percentage of ballots cast in early voting, voter turnout increased .07 percent.[17] In an election where nearly 25 percent of voters voted early, turnout increased by less than 2 percent.

Richardson and Neeley found that early voting in Tennessee's 1994 election produced a positive effect on turnout of 9 percent.[18] A recent study by Smith and Comer shows that early voting had a negative effect on turnout.[19] Comparing states with early voting to states without it, Curtis Gans has mixed findings. On the whole, he reports, early voting "hurts turnout," but in several midterm elections early-voting states increased their turnout more than other states. In presidential years, Gans found the opposite.[20]

Gronke finds that early voting does not increase voter turnout. As was observed with absentee and mail balloting, low-turnout elections show higher turnout with early voting, but more prominent elections do not, and they do not attract new voters on the state or county level.[21]

Stein, Leighley, and Owens sum up by noting that, "simply put, in-person early voting has been used by those who otherwise would have been most likely to vote on Election Day."[22]

Convenience in Voting

Despite the evident failure of absentee and early voting to increase turnout rates significantly, it is worthwhile to consider the convenience of these methods. People like convenience in voting, and they cite reasons of inconvenience as obstacles to voting. Convenience could mean a happier electorate and make it easier for many to vote without the disruption to their lives sometimes imposed by election day polling-place voting. While convenience for voters is not as compelling a reason for promoting absentee and early voting, it is a good in itself.

The Popularity of Voting before Election Day

From early on, Oregonians have expressed confidence in their vote-by-mail system. In the 1998 referendum that moved Oregon to vote by mail for all elections, 70 percent supported it.[23] Prior to the referendum, surveys showed that nearly 80 percent favored vote-by-mail over polling-place voting, and a similar percentage found it more convenient.[24] Results from a 2003 survey were very similar, with 80.9 percent preferring vote-by-mail as opposed to only 19.1 percent preferring polling-place voting.[25] In 1997, a survey in Washington State showed that 65 percent preferred voting by mail.[26] The popularity of early voting in Texas has also been reported by some researchers, although the evidence is mostly anecdotal.[27]

A recent national poll on voting convenience was commissioned by the Why Tuesday group (whytuesday.org), which favors moving election day to a weekend. Ninety-four percent of respondents said they believed society should make it "as convenient as possible for eligible citizens to vote," and 58 percent agreed that "Congress should work to make voting easier to do."[28]

As for specific methods of convenience voting, 57 percent favored "early voting with no reason needed so that anyone could vote at a designated location for twenty-one days prior to the election," while "voting via the mail for a period of several weeks before the election" was favored by 56 percent. Respondents were also relatively closely split on, but with slight majorities opposed to, making election day a national holiday or moving it to the weekend.[29]

Inconvenience as an Obstacle to Voting

Bolstering the argument that Americans care about convenience are survey data on the reasons Americans give for not voting.

TABLE 3-1
PERCENTAGE DISTRIBUTION OF REASONS FOR NOT VOTING

	1998	2000	2002	2004
Illness or Disability	11.1	14.8	13.1	15.4
Out of Town	8.3	10.2	10.4	9.0
Forgot to Vote	5.3	4.0	5.7	3.4
Not Interested	12.7	12.2	12.0	10.7
Too Busy, Conflicting Schedule	34.9	20.9	27.1	19.9
Transportation Problems	1.8	2.4	1.7	2.1
Did Not Like Candidates or Campaign Issues	5.5	7.7	7.3	9.9
Registration Problems	3.6	6.9	4.1	6.8
Bad Weather	0.2	0.6	0.7	0.5
Inconvenient Polling Place	1.1	2.6	1.4	3.0
Other Reason	8.3	10.2	9.0	10.9
Don't Know or Refused	7.1	7.5	7.5	8.5

SOURCE: U.S. Census Bureau, *Current Population Survey*, November 1998, 2000, 2002, and 2004, http://www.census.gov/population/www/socdemo/voting.html (accessed August 24, 2006).

Recent Census Bureau surveys have asked nonvoters the reason they did not vote. Some of the open-ended responses fall under the category of political disengagement, such as those reported by respondents who did not like the candidates, forgot to vote, or were not interested. A number of reasons, however, were related to convenience in voting.

In the presidential elections of 2000 and 2004, about 20 percent of nonvoters said that they were too busy or had something on their schedules conflicting with voting (see table 3-1). Between 9 and 10 percent said they did not vote because they were out of town, while 14–15 percent said they were ill or disabled. Finally, relatively small numbers cited bad weather, inconvenient polling places, and transportation problems.[30]

Absentee or early voting could conceivably alleviate several obstacles cited by nonvoters. Presumably, the option to vote in an early voting period of several days or by absentee would mitigate problems such as lack of transportation, bad weather, and inconvenient polling places, although these were cited by a relatively small number of nonvoters.

Pre–election-day voting might also be of some modest help to the larger group of nonvoters who cited illness and being out of town. State laws allow most people who are out of town or sick to cast absentee ballots, but the survey response indicates there are situations not easily addressed by this provision. Take for example, sudden out-of-town trips or illnesses. Pre–election-day voting might help in some of these circumstances, as it might be more convenient than some states' procedures for requesting absentee ballots, but it would do little to deal with last-minute emergencies for voters who have not voted early.

Presumably, preelection voting would be most helpful to the 20 percent of nonvoters who did not vote because they were too busy or had a scheduling conflict. A longer period of voting would clear up some conflicts. It is worth noting, however, that nonvoters cited these reasons at substantially higher rates in midterm elections than in presidential elections. This seems to indicate that being busy is relative to the importance of the election. A busy person might feel a greater obligation to vote in a presidential election than a midterm.

The Census Bureau responses by nonvoters point indirectly to the issue of voter convenience. It is likely that many voters encountered some of the same difficulties as nonvoters, but they were able to overcome them and cast votes. Some people who were busy, ill, or out of town, or who were faced with transportation problems, inconvenient polling places, or bad weather, nonetheless voted. For them these were just inconveniences, not obstacles to voting.

Finally, one recent study shows that early voting in particular is used by those for whom convenience is especially important: voters who are politically sophisticated, and who live at the fringes of large cities. They are savvy enough to know that early voting is an alternative to election-day voting, and harried enough with their commutes and busy lives to want to take advantage of it. This same research shows that these types of early voters are likely to spread the word to similarly situated citizens, thereby increasing the use of early-voting polling places.[31]

Given the large percentage of nonvoters who cite inconvenience as a reason for not voting, it is understandable why some advocates of absentee and early voting believe these methods will increase turnout. Remove the obstacles, the reasoning goes, and nonvoters will vote. But the academic literature shows little or no increase in voter turnout with the adoption of early and absentee voting. It is conceivable that the convenience of voting before election day increases turnout among some who face obstacles, while decreasing turnout for other reasons—for instance, as a result of the lessened intensity of an election spread out over time. But it is interesting to note that despite the great increase in national rates of absentee and early voting from 2000 to 2004, the percentage of respondents who were busy remained the same.

Conclusion

Convenience, not voter turnout, is the chief benefit of absentee, mail, and early voting. Voters tend to like their new preelection options for voting. Convenience is popular, and inconvenience is cited as a reason for not voting by a significant proportion of nonvoters.

For voter turnout, the benefits of absentee, mail, and early voting are minimal. Large, positive turnout effects are seen only in very low-turnout local elections, and these could be attained in other ways—by combining local elections with statewide elections on the same voting day, for instance. This would be especially effective if states kept their ballots relatively short to prevent voter drop-off. Or states might use mail voting only for small elections, although this entails maintaining several voting systems. While some very modest positive turnout effects are seen in mail and early elections other than local ones, these methods do not seem to attract new voters; rather, they retain a slightly larger share of sometime-voters.

It would be easy to dismiss convenience because it seems less important than voter turnout. But given the great rise in preelection voting and its popularity, convenience is a worthwhile objective, and one that voters will continue to insist on.

The early reformers who introduced absentee ballots were concerned that classes of people were effectively disenfranchised because they could not vote at local polling places on election day. Because those early reformers fought and won those battles, the absentee ballot is available today to almost everyone who cannot make it to the polls. Liberalized absentee voting, voting by mail, and early voting will not, however, extend the vote to effectively disenfranchised citizens, as absentee voting was originally intended to do for Civil War soldiers in the field and away from home who could not possibly cast a ballot. What these forms of pre–election-day voting accomplish is to give more choices to voters and to make it easier for them to fit voting into their busy lives.

4

The Pitfalls of Absentee and Early Voting

The move to increase absentee and early voting has been driven by a desire to make voting more convenient. Even though the vast body of academic research shows that convenience voting makes little or no impact on voter turnout, the aim of facilitating the vote for those who find it difficult to get to an election-day voting booth is a laudable one.

As we have seen, the task of the reformers who first introduced absentee voting was more urgent than today's calls for greater convenience in voting. Before the absentee ballot, certain people like soldiers in the field or railroad workers were unable to vote, so adoption of absentee voting was a necessity for them.

Today, almost every eligible American has an opportunity to vote, but reformers worry that there are obstacles to voting—not insurmountable ones, but discouragements nonetheless. Why not, say reformers, make voting easier for the elderly, the busy single working mom, or the person living in a rural area far from a polling station?

It is tempting to say that the motivations of the early reformers were superior to and of a wholly different kind than those of today's advocates of preelection voting. But, in truth, they hold a great deal in common. Both were and are interested in removing obstacles placed in the way of voting. Both were and are problem-solvers, advocating real-world solutions to help citizens vote.

The great difference between the two is a question of balance. Even though the stakes were very high during the Civil War and at the beginning of the twentieth century, proponents of the absentee ballot tried to balance the access to the vote with their concerns about the integrity of the ballot.

Only this balancing of priorities explains how the procedures for voting by absentee ballot came about. In most states, voters were asked to provide an acceptable reason for voting absentee, and they were expected to go before a notary public with a blank ballot and then proceed to fill it out—not so the notary could see a voter's choices, but rather could attest to the fact that the ballot had been cast freely. The notary might also be able to weed out someone who would impersonate another voter, or seek to cast a ballot for a dead or nonexistent person.

Today, the motivation to remove obstacles to voting is often not balanced with concerns about the integrity of the ballot, the protection of the secret ballot, and other goods that derive from voting at an election-day polling place.

This chapter will examine the problems of absentee and early voting. The first part will consider the potential for fraud and coercion in absentee voting. It will also examine the troubling role of intermediaries in the absentee-ballot process. Finally, it will consider the worst-case scenario of absentee-ballot fraud corrupting an election.

The second part of the chapter will consider two problems raised by both absentee and early voting. As both occur before election day, they threaten to undermine the civic character of a single election day, and they raise the possibility of voters casting votes without having all the information provided by a full election campaign.

Fraud and Coercion and Absentee Ballots

Vote fraud is difficult to detect, to measure accurately, and to prove. The discussion of the importance of fraud can also be politically divisive, as in the current controversy over whether states should require photo ID cards at polling places.

There is little evidence of systematic and widespread election fraud. Those concerned with voter fraud do not claim that it threatens to undermine every election across the country. Conspiracies to alter the outcomes of elections are not lurking around every corner.

In fact, common sense tells us that the incentives to commit election fraud are only significant in somewhat competitive elections where the fraud might have a chance of affecting the outcome of the race. Given the great number of uncompetitive federal, state, and local elections in the United States, the concern is not that fraud is widespread, but that it is possible, and that if it were to occur it would not only undermine the results of a particular election, but would undermine confidence in elections in general.

On the other side of this argument are those who believe voter fraud is a small problem, especially when compared to the bad effects of trying to crack down on it excessively. The requirement of photo identification at the polling place is where this debate reaches a fever pitch, with proponents finding it necessary to verify that only eligible voters are voting, and opponents arguing that because not everyone possesses photo ID, such a law would disenfranchise many.

While there will always be disagreement over the seriousness of election fraud in general, both sides to this argument agree on one important matter: The most likely avenue for voter fraud is absentee balloting, which offers more opportunities for it than the traditional polling place.

Spencer Overton, for example, a member of the Carter-Baker Commission on Federal Election Reform, argued strenuously against and ultimately publicly dissented from the commission's recommendation to require photo identification at the polling place. In the course of his argument, he noted that the commission had its fraud protections backwards, because it was satisfied with a check of a voter's signature for absentee ballots but would ultimately require a photo ID at the polling place. The Carter-Baker plan, he wrote,

> proposes that voters be able to verify their identity [at the polling place] using a signature match, but it would eliminate that option after 2009 while recommending a permanent signature match for absentee voters. This double standard is particularly disturbing because whites are much more likely than blacks to

vote absentee, *and because the potential for fraud is greater with absentee ballots* [emphasis mine].[1]

John Fund, who is on the other side of the photo ID debate and is generally concerned with the possibility of fraud in the electoral system, also agrees that the most serious opportunities for fraud are presented by absentee voting: "Absentee ballots," he says, "represent the biggest source of potential election fraud because of the way they are obtained and voted."[2]

Susceptibility of Absentee Votes to Fraud

The main reason absentee ballots are susceptible to fraud is the separation of both ballot and voter from the polling place, with all of its integrity and privacy protections.

At a polling place today, the ballot is secure. Voters must present themselves and at least declare who they are in person. In many states, they may have to show a form of identification. The ballot is not to be handled by poll workers, other voters, party officials, spouses, relatives, or companions of the voter. The voter casts or deposits the ballot without assistance, in a privacy booth or curtained stall that allows him or her to do so in complete secrecy. No one can influence the voter while voting, nor see the completed ballot.[3]

Absentee ballots have none of these protections. The early reformers tried to address the problem by requiring that voters provide approved reasons to vote absentee and find a notary public who would attest to the fact that the ballot was cast freely.[4] Even so, fraud could not be avoided. From the earliest use of absentee ballots, these questions of security have been raised. During the Civil War, agents of Horatio Seymour, Democratic governor of New York, were charged with entering hospitals where soldiers had been admitted, impersonating the soldiers, forging their names, and casting ballots for them.[5]

Similar fraud occurs today. In 2005, a Connecticut state representative admitted that he "illegally induced elderly residents of the Betty Knox housing complex in Hartford to cast absentee ballots for him."[6] And, in connection with the closely contested Washington State governor's race in 2004, two people were prosecuted in King County for having cast absentee ballots for their deceased spouses. This was not widespread corruption. Both admitted to having cast the ballots in honor of their spouses. Even so, neither forged signature was caught by election officials at the time, so the votes were counted.[7]

To cite yet another case, John Fund, in his book on election fraud, describes some of the problems with the Miami mayoral election of 1998. A number of voters were paid to vote. One elderly political boss was found with over one hundred absentee ballots in his home.[8] And recently, in Wise County, Virginia, three elected officials were charged with over nine hundred counts of voter fraud. The major charges were that they had filled out absentee ballot applications for other citizens, intercepted the ballots in the mail, and voted the ballots for their preferred candidates.[9]

Absentee Ballots and Coercion

Absentee ballots leave open the possibility of voter coercion. While there is no indication that coercion is any more widespread than fraud, without the privacy protections of the voting booth, absentee voters could be subject to other parties pressuring them to vote a particular way. And as the ballot is potentially available for anyone to see, the perpetrator of coercion can ensure it is cast "properly," unlike at a polling place, where a voter can promise his associates he will vote one way but then go behind the privacy curtain and vote his conscience.

One recent example involved outright vote-buying. In an East Chicago mayoral race in 2003, the challenger had beaten the incumbent in the polling-place vote but ended up losing the election based on the absentee vote. The challenger's volunteers uncovered instances of absentee fraud, including that of a woman who allowed a campaign worker to fill out her ballot in exchange for a $100 job at the polls. One hundred fifty-five absentee ballots were ultimately thrown out, although this was not enough to change the outcome of the election.[10]

Coercion can also take the form of an individual threatening another to "properly fill out the ballot." This might include the subtle coercion of a husband who wants to make sure his wife has not made any mistakes on her ballot. Absentee ballots can also be subject to pressure from a citizen's company or union. Take the case of a "helpful" ballot-filling-out party, where likeminded workers get together to talk about issues and complete their ballots. Of course, since the absentee ballot has left the privacy of the polling place, all of an attending voter's colleagues may be able to see how he voted and express approval or disapproval.

Role of Third-Party Intermediaries in Absentee Ballots

As we have seen, Eric Oliver's study of voter turnout and absentee voting found that the use of no-excuses absentee ballots did not in itself cause a rise in turnout in the elections he looked at, but that turnout rose when no-excuses absentee balloting was combined with political party mobilization. In particular, he cited party officials sending completed absentee ballot applications to prospective voters of their parties.[11]

The connection between the political parties' "get out the vote" efforts and preelection voting is becoming a significant factor in elections. In 2004, both parties knew the possibilities for early and absentee voting in each state and used them to their advantage. For example, President George W. Bush, in a taped phone message to Wisconsin Republicans, urged them to vote absentee. The Democratic Party in Iowa was adept at encouraging its voters to cast absentee ballots. Starting in the summer, party volunteers would call party voters to encourage them to vote absentee. If a voter agreed, a volunteer would show up at the voter's door that day with the ballot application.[12]

It is in the interest of both parties to lock as many of their voters in as they can before election day. Why risk the possibility that loyal voters will not go to the polls on election day when you can secure their votes early? In the fall of 2004, Iowa Democratic chairman Gordon Fischer argued, "We've got to bank as many votes as possible before November 2."[13]

In addition to the political parties themselves, other groups encouraged preelection voting in 2004. The independent Democratic-leaning group America Coming Together (ACT), for example, made a substantial effort to get Democratic voters to vote before election day. The head of the group, Jim Jordan, indicated that ACT had "thousands and thousands of employees going door to door in the battleground states and they talk to virtually everyone about early voting and vote-by-mail." Jordan's reason for this echoed the sentiment of party operatives that loyal voters should be locked in: "One of the primary advantages is simply to bank votes—better to have the bird in the hand."[14]

Clint Reed, who worked on the Republican Party's campaign in Arkansas in 2004, indicated another advantage for parties. If they can lock in loyal voters early, they can then dedicate more resources to other voters in the last few days of the campaign: "You can spend the last 72 hours of your campaign, or the last 96 hours, or the last two weeks, focusing on those independent swing voters."[15]

Laws with respect to the handling of absentee ballots vary widely from state to state, but there have been troubling cases of third-party misdeeds. Michael Moss reported in the *New York Times* that it was becoming a common practice for the parties to hold absentee ballots before turning them in to county registrars for processing. The stated reason for doing so is to time voting messages and advertisements to the arrival of absentee ballots in voters' hands. A county judge in Arizona found that a campaign consultant had held onto fourteen thousand absentee-ballot applications.[16] There are also serious concerns that campaign workers might pick up absentee ballots from voters but only selectively turn some in for processing.

Overall, the parties have many incentives to act as intermediaries in procuring absentee ballots, but there are troubling questions about their involvement.

Disqualifying Absentee Ballots

The consequences of fraud associated with absentee voting have occasionally gone beyond the particular ballots affected. In two Florida elections, the problems were so deep that a judge threw out all of the absentee ballots in one case and the whole election in the other.

In a very close Miami mayoral race in 1998, absentee votes provided the margin of victory for Xavier Suarez over Joe Carrollo. But such rampant absentee-ballot fraud was discovered that a judge ended up throwing out all of the absentee ballots—over four thousand—and handing the election to Carollo.[17] In 1993, in Hialeah, Florida, a judge called a new election because the absentee ballots were tainted.

Protections against Fraud for Absentee Ballots

There are two primary protections against fraud in absentee ballots. First, the Help America Vote Act now requires that someone who both registers and votes by mail must at some point show up in person with identification—something that could be avoided in some states prior to the act's passage in 2002. The concern addressed by the act was, of course, that fictitious names would be registered and absentee ballots cast on their behalf.

The second protection against fraud is the signature check. Unfortunately, according to John Mark Hansen, former director of the National Commission on Federal Election Reform co-chaired by former presidents Gerald Ford and Jimmy Carter, "For practical reasons, most states do not routinely check signatures either on applications or on returned ballots, just as most states do not verify signatures or require proof of identity at the polls."[18] This raises questions not only about absentee ballots, but also regarding protections against fraud at the polling place, although there has been a recent move by states to institute identification requirements.

Oregon votes essentially 100 percent by mail, so it is subject to some of the same concerns as high-absentee states. But Oregon has an advantage over other high-absentee states in preventing fraud, in part because of the nature of its system, and in part because of the state's own good practices. Oregon does not avoid all potential for fraud, but it has done a good job compared to its counterparts.

Paul Gronke surveyed practices of election officials in Oregon aimed at reducing the possibility of fraud. First, Gronke noted, Oregon, unlike every other state, has essentially a unitary system. It does not have to maintain a polling-place voting system or an early-voting system; it votes totally by mail.[19] Because of this, Oregon election officials are good at what they do. For the same reason, Oregon does not have to deal with the problem of monitoring voters who might, for example, try to vote absentee and then show up in person on election day.[20]

Second, Gronke tells us, Oregon has a universal signature check. Every ballot is checked for a signature match, poll workers are required to undergo training in signature identification, and there are procedures for resolving disputed signatures. And third, as Oregon has a vote-by-mail system, it mails ballots directly to voters. Voters do not apply for their ballots; they receive them if they are registered. There is no place for intermediaries to apply for or deliver ballots to voters, and the state does not allow them to be forwarded through the mail. If undeliverable, they must be returned to the state, which can use that information to update their voting records.[21]

While its delivery of the vote-by-mail ballots is less susceptible to fraud than traditional absentee ballots, Oregon still has had a problem with drop-off sites for ballots. Since the voter must return the ballot to Oregon, it could potentially be intercepted by a third party, or political parties might act as intermediaries delivering ballots to drop-off sites.

In his study, Gronke expressed concern about unofficial drop-off boxes (many of which are probably legitimate); subsequently, the state legislature passed legislation to deal with the problem.[22] And while Oregon's signature check is more thorough than other states', it is not clear if fraud involving forgeries and impersonations would be detected.

Loss of Civic Day of Election

There is no doubt that we have moved significantly away from holding a single election day in many states. A civic day when the community comes together to make important public decisions has psychological value for the nation.

But there are two further, related reasons to lament the loss of such a day. First, research has shown that in addition to thinking about the obstacles that prevent people from voting, we should consider the positives that bring people to the polls. A body of research has developed to identify factors that prompt citizens to vote. Donald Green and Alan Gerber have conducted many experiments in contacting voters with an eye to getting them to the polls. They have found that voter contact does increase turnout rates. Mail and phone banks can have an effect, but the effect is more pronounced when there are multiple personal contacts coming from people within the community. Or, as Green and Gerber put it, "A personal approach to mobilizing voters is generally more effective than an impersonal approach."[23] Related research by Green and others is looking at election-day parties near the polling place as a way to increase turnout. Very preliminary results also showed a positive effect. This finding again underscores the positive value of a celebrated, community-oriented election. The work on the positive draws to voting could indicate turnout will drop off if voters have a longer period of time to vote or have to cast a vote in an impersonal manner. Or, at least, it might indicate that alternatives to election-day voting should incorporate a personal aspect.

A second, related value of a single, civic election day is its intensity. Gans emphasizes this point in two ways. First, voter interest might wane in an extended voting period. Second, the institutions that turn out voters might be less well-mobilized over a longer, less intense period. We have seen that parties are adapting to new early- and absentee-voting procedures, so a longer election period is certainly not discouraging voter mobilization. But it may be that both voter interest and turnout efforts might be more effective on a single day or for a shorter period.

Voting before the Campaign Has Ended

In addition to diminishing the civic character of a single election day, the ability to vote early may lead substantial numbers of voters to miss out on important information in the campaign. This is an issue with both absentee and early voting, but for the former in particular, as absentee-voting periods are almost always longer than those for early voting. Bolstering this concern is evidence that voting more than a week before the election is on the rise. But it is still true that most pre–election-day voters vote in the week before the election, and those who cast their votes early tend to be more partisan, more knowledgeable about issues, and less subject to campaign persuasion. Despite these caveats, a shorter period of pre–election-day voting would minimize the loss of election day as a civic day and would mean that fewer voters would miss out on important campaign information.

Conclusion

Absentee ballots are subject to a number of fraud and coercion issues not relevant to polling-place voting. Early voting at a polling place does not produce as many troubling questions as absentee voting. Many people make use of absentee and early voting, and it is unlikely these methods will wither away. The challenge is to balance the good that comes with the convenience of preelection voting with the worries about fraud that accompany absentee balloting in particular.

The separation of absentee ballots from the polling place raises apprehensions about the forging of signatures, the manipulation of elderly voters, and the handling of ballots by third parties, including the political parties. Absentee voters can be pressured by their spouses, unions, companies, friends, or social groups. There have even been cases of all of the absentee ballots from an election being disqualified, and of an entire election being rerun because of doubts about the integrity of the absentee ballots.

Early voting is not subject to many of these issues, because the ballot never leaves the polling place. However, both absentee voting and early voting are subject to two concerns: first, that the move to more pre–election-day voting will diminish election day as a civic day, and, second, that voting before election day might make some voters miss the full course of the campaign and thus prevent them from hearing as much as they should from the candidates.

With regard to the civic day, there is a practical concern that voting before election day might spread the election too thin over too extended a period. This might make voter mobilization more difficult and dampen voter interest, especially for states whose early and absentee voting begins over six weeks before the election.

The question of voters missing out on important information in the campaign by voting early is a particular concern for absentee voting, where ballots can be mailed to voters at least forty-five days before an election. It is true that most absentee and early polling place voters cast their ballots in the week before the election, and that those who vote early tend to be more partisan, more knowledgeable about issues, and less subject to campaign persuasion. Even so, there have been troubling signs of a trend toward voting even earlier. A shorter period of pre–election-day voting would mean that fewer voters would miss important campaign information, and it would minimize the loss of election day as a civic day as well.

Conclusions and Recommendations

Voting in America has undergone a major transformation in the past twenty-five years. Large numbers of voters cast their ballots before election day, either through the mail or at early-voting polling places. While the change has been dramatic, with pre–election-day voting rising from about 5 percent of votes cast in 1980 to over 20 percent in 2004, it has been effected somewhat silently, incrementally, state by state, and without a national debate.

In 2004, the national rate of absentee voting comprised approximately 15 percent of all votes, while early voting accounted for roughly 7 percent. It is likely that both will continue to increase. There is about twice as much absentee as early voting, but early voting appears to be increasing at a faster rate.

The Effects of Large-Scale Voting before Election Day

While the trend toward more voting in advance of election day is clear, the effects of such a change are not easily foreseen. The great promise of voting before election day is that it will make voting more convenient and increase voter turnout. There is no doubt that these methods add a level of convenience to the voting process, and voters tend to favor the flexibility they offer. But the evidence for increased turnout is thin. At best, absentee or mail voting may help turnout in very low-turnout elections. For more prominent elections, any increase is modest—a few percentage points at most—and is drawn from higher turnout by habitual voters, not from new voters.

Other possible benefits of early and absentee voting that are beyond the scope of this study include lower cost as compared to traditional voting, and the capacity to allow states to spread resources more evenly across the state. These methods may also alleviate shortages of poll workers and improve the counting of ballots.

With these arguments in favor of voting in advance of election day come real concerns. While irregularities may occur in traditional polling-place voting, absentee and mail ballots have special problems with respect to fraud and coercion. A ballot that arrives in the mail cannot be cast with the same protections as those afforded by the polling place, where voters cast their votes alone and privately, and where no one can observe their choices. There are no curtains around absentee voters, and no poll workers or public officials to ensure that an absentee ballot is cast freely and secretly.

When a ballot arrives in the mail, there is nothing to stop a nosy spouse, unscrupulous boss, or other shady character from seeking to coerce the voter into casting it for a particular candidate or cause. It is hard to regulate the participation of intermediaries who might request ballots for or deliver ballots to voters, attempt to return ballots for voters, or, in the worst cases, "assist" vulnerable voters in filling out ballots, or even fill ballots out for them without their knowledge. While most states have laws governing abuses of absentee ballots, many allow assistance in requesting and returning them. Many states also allow the political parties to play a role, requesting ballots for voters or, at minimum, encouraging voters to vote absentee.

Voter fraud of any kind devalues the votes of legitimate voters. If ballots are cast for dead or fictional people, the vote of legitimate voters is worth less and may even be invalidated completely, as in the Miami mayoral election where a judge decided that fraud was so pervasive that all the absentee ballots had to be thrown out. Such fraud is exceptionally difficult to prove or measure, and in absentee voting, where the ballots are separated from the privacy of the polling place, and where third parties play a great role, the potential for fraud is especially serious.

Finally, there have recently been several troubling developments in absentee voting. In particular, among their otherwise laudable efforts to ease voting for overseas military troops, several states have allowed faxed ballots, which would seem to be especially susceptible to fraud. Also, there have been calls for Internet voting, which, if allowed, would raise technical security concerns as well as the privacy concerns already presented by absentee ballots.

As with absentee voting, studies of early voting have not consistently shown an increase in turnout, but there is evidence that people believe this option will make voting more convenient for them. In addition, an early voting period would likely cover at least one weekend before the election and increase voting opportunities for those who have a hard time getting to the polls on a workday.

Early voting does not present all of the same problems as absentee balloting, as it does not separate the ballot from the polling place. Early voters can cast their votes in the privacy of a voting booth, and there are no intermediaries in the process. Because early voting is a relatively new phenomenon, however, it has not always been implemented with the same protections as election-day polling-place voting. Florida, for instance, instituted early voting without enacting rules forbidding solicitation of votes within a certain number of feet from the polling location, like those that protect election-day voters from harassment by partisans and from pressure from those who would seek to influence their votes.

Two other issues are raised by both early and absentee voting. First, when people cast their votes prior to election day, they do not have the benefit of hearing the entire campaign and may vote before key information is revealed by the candidates. In 2004, when the presidential debates were held from September 30 to October 13, early voting began in Tennessee on October 13, before the last debate took place. Oregon mailed its ballots out in late September, before any of the debates. Other last-minute events and final messages put out in television ads and speeches by candidates' campaigns may also be missed by a significant fraction of a public that votes early.

The second issue is the status of election day as a civic day of voting. A large amount of absentee and early voting takes away from the notion that there is one day on which everyone displays a civic pride by going to the polls. A single election day emphasizes that while voting is an individual activity, it is also part of a larger communal exercise. In addition to its symbolic importance, such a day also may serve to remind Americans of the importance of the right to vote and may encourage voting. A related concern is the potential loss of the mechanisms for turning out voters and of the urgency of voting that surrounds a single election day. This concern applies to those who vote early at polling places, but even more so to absentee voters, who typically have a longer period of time before election day to cast their votes.

Recommendations

The rise in early and absentee voting is proceeding at a rapid pace, and it is impossible to imagine that such trends will stop or reverse themselves in the future. Given that reality, I offer two types of recommendations to improve a quickly changing system and address the concerns raised by the increasingly common use of these methods. First, I offer a global—or, more accurately, a national—recommendation for a viable model of polling-place, early, and absentee voting. Second, given that early and absentee voting varies widely from state to state, I present recommendations that are tailored to particular categories of states: low-absentee states, high-absentee states, states with high early voting, and mixed absentee- and early-voting states.

General Recommendations. Despite the increase in early and absentee voting, the election-day polling place should continue to be the central touchstone of elections. The 2000 Florida presidential election controversy led to the 2002 passage of the Help America Vote Act, which is beginning to reshape the polling-place experience. States are in the process of replacing outdated vote-casting devices and instituting computerized, statewide registration databases, and they have already established provisional voting, which allows voters whose names do not appear on registration lists to cast votes and to have those votes subsequently counted if it can be shown that the voter should have been on the list.

A model for voting should include the complete implementation of such polling-place reforms, as well as place an additional emphasis on making the experience at the polling place a good one for voters. In particular, states should extend their hours at polling places from at least 6 a.m. to 9 p.m. to accommodate those who vote before, during, and after the typical workday. States must also dedicate greater resources to the recruitment and training of poll workers.

As an additional way to improve polling-place voting, states should study and possibly adopt forms of vote centers that have been implemented in a number of counties, particularly Larimer County, Colorado. These large vote centers replace many small precinct polling places, allow voters in the county to cast their votes at any of them, and are located along heavily trafficked commuter routes. Early research has shown that Larimer-style vote centers did increase turnout and bring in new voters.[1]

In addition to improving the election-day polling place, states should institute a short period of early voting, preferably from five to seven days, but no longer than ten days. Voters should not have to provide a reason for voting early at a polling place. The early-voting period should not commence until after the final candidate debates or major public candidate forums have taken place. To ensure that the most relevant political information gets to voters in advance of their casting their votes, states have a responsibility to keep their early-voting periods reasonably short, and organizations that sponsor candidate events should schedule them in advance of the early-voting period. Early-voting sites must also have the same protections as polling places, with the same restrictions on solicitation within a certain distance and the same presence of poll workers and observers. In addition, the hours for early voting should hew as closely as possible to the ideal election-day polling hours, allowing votes to be cast on weekends and before, during, and after typical working hours.

With the introduction of an early-voting period, states must adopt rules on ballot integrity to ensure that ballots and machines are secured each day and are not susceptible to tampering. This is a difficult task, not only because of the number of days that ballots must be secured, but also because some early-voting centers may cut across precincts, and the tallies from them will have to be merged with election-day and absentee returns. States must also ensure, with the help of new statewide databases, that the several systems of voting (election day, early, and absentee) do not allow citizens to vote more than once.

Absentee voting will be a necessary part of any state's voting system, as there are people who will not be able to get to an election-day or early-voting polling place. But with improved hours and conditions on election day, and with an early-voting period of reasonable length, the number of people who must vote by absentee ballot will be small. Additional measures that should be taken include the following:

- To discourage unnecessary absentee voting and encourage would-be absentee voters to take advantage of early voting, states should ask voters to state a reason for using an absentee ballot and grant permanent absentee status only to those who indicate valid reasons for needing it, such as long-term disability or relocation overseas.

- States should consider reintroducing witness requirements. While appearing before a notary public might be too great an inconvenience to absentee voters, a signature by two witnesses should not prove to be a great burden. And states should limit the number of absentee votes to which any one person can serve as a witness in order to prevent organized efforts to coerce voters.

- States should not allow third parties to request or be involved with the dissemination, transport, or collection of absentee ballots.

- When considering voter identification requirements for polling-place voters, states should also reconsider their identification requirements for absentee voters. The signature-check system that presently governs most absentee balloting should be audited and improved. States should check the signatures on 100 percent of absentee ballots, as Oregon does with its vote-by-mail system. They should also study technology that supplements human checking of signatures.

- States should make efforts to improve communication with absentee voters to indicate that their ballots have been received and counted. Additionally, rules regarding receipt of ballots through the military mail should be improved so that overseas personnel can learn whether their ballots have been counted.

- States must firmly adhere to the rule of mailing out ballots forty-five days in advance to overseas voters, and they should ensure that their primary election days are scheduled to make this possible.

- Finally, while striving to improve the experience of overseas military voters, states should not adopt fax ballots, which could easily lead to fraud. The Department of Defense should also eschew Internet voting, and instead spend its resources improving the absentee system for its personnel.

One other area that must be addressed with reference to early and absentee voting regards the issues of horserace polling and media reports of early results. A number of European countries—France and Italy, for example—ban public opinion polling directly before elections. The rationale behind such a rule is that last-minute polling might affect voter decisions. With no such rule in the United States, polling and the public release of polls continue up to election day, so that over 20 percent of our citizens cast their ballots in the midst of a flood of polls. It is hard to imagine a ban on polling similar to those of European countries, but given the large number of votes cast before election day, an agreement by media organizations and those who set standards for professional polling could discourage polling at least in the last few days before an election.

More problematic are exit polls and their release. On election day, partial results are released throughout the day to media members of a consortium. Washington insiders see it as a game to get these early partial results and pretend to have greater knowledge of the outcome than the general public. With so much early voting taking place, exit polls are also likely to be conducted earlier and partial results privately released to media organizations in advance of election day. There is a danger that the early results will get out and affect perceptions of an ongoing election. Media organizations and the firms they hire to conduct exit polls should agree not to have any private pre–election-day releases of partial results.

Finally, states should engage in greater communication with voters. First, written communications sent by mail should clearly let voters know whether they are on registration lists and where their polling places and early-voting sites are, and more states should adopt and disseminate the voter guides that have been popular in Oregon and Washington State. Research has shown that frequent government contact with voters may increase turnout, and it cannot help but to improve voter education.

While such written and also electronic communication with voters is helpful, research shows that face-to-face contact has more effect. Despite the expense such contact will entail, states, as well as the political parties, should be proactive in this way to reach some voters in person.

Specific Recommendations. The foregoing general recommendations are based on the assumption that we are never going back to the days of less than 5 percent absentee voting, provided only for those with a proven need. However, different states begin in very different places, and their journeys to a voting system involving extensive absentee and early voting will be varied. Because of the great variety of approaches toward these methods, the following specific recommendations are offered for the different categories of states, as described in chapter 2.

Recommendations for Low-Absentee States. Nearly half of the states are still traditional, low-absentee-voting states. For them, the dangers of large amounts of absentee voting seem remote. But it is striking how quickly a state can change from a low-absentee state to one where absentee voting is relatively common. Take, for example, Florida, which in 2000 would have been characterized as a low-absentee state, with less than 15 percent of voters casting absentee ballots. With the introduction of early voting, Florida in 2004 had 18.7 percent vote early, plus 17.5 percent vote absentee. States that adopt a significant program of early voting often find they have rates of early voting well over 10 percent at the first major election after the change. But even states with more encouraging laws and attitudes toward it may find that, over a relatively short period of time, absentee voting becomes a large proportion of the vote. Iowa, for example, in 1988 had only 6.5 percent of its votes cast absentee, and in 2004 had over 30 percent.

Changes in voting procedures may also come about in sudden or unexpected ways. The initiative process, for example, may effect a quick and likely irrevocable change in voting procedures. In 2005, for example, Ohio had a referendum on whether to introduce no-excuses absentee balloting. While this initiative was rejected, it raises the possibility that an expansion of early or absentee voting may appear suddenly on the political radar screen and be quickly enacted without detailed consideration of how it will affect a state's overall conduct of elections.

For this reason, it would be wise for states to consider their long-term futures in voting. Specifically, low-absentee states should adopt the following measures:

- Introduce modest forms of early voting. These should be limited in time, and, perhaps at first, limited to county clerks' offices. This experiment could be accompanied by a message of encouragement to vote early rather than absentee. Such a trial would allow election officials the opportunity to see if early voting works well in their states, and whether they should continue with it or slowly expand it. Officials should also be mindful that early-voting polling stations have protections identical to those of election-day facilities, such as the same requirement for poll workers, the same zone of nonsolicitation near the polling place, and so forth.

- Resist calls for no-excuses absentee voting (which almost all high-absentee states have), and permanent absentee status. States should at least limit such status to voters who have long-term reasons for voting absentee, such as those serving in official capacities overseas and the permanently disabled or frail. They should also be wary of changes in laws and procedures that would encourage the participation of political parties and other third parties in the procurement of absentee ballots.

- Make election-day polling places more accessible by extending polling hours at least from 6 a.m. to 9 p.m. on election day, and ensure that early-voting sites have the same hours and polling-place protections as election-day polling locations.

Recommendations for High-Absentee States. States with high rates of absentee voting would have to make the most significant changes in their systems to conform with the general recommendations laid out above. Absentee voting has become part of the culture in these states, popular with voters and expected. It is hard to imagine that such attitudes will change.

There are two distinct classes of high-absentee states. In one group are Oregon, which has 100 percent mail voting, and Washington State, which has nearly 70 percent absentee voting and severe pressures on it to move to an all-mail voting system. The issues facing these two states are different from those facing California, Arizona, and other states where absentee ballot rates are high, but not yet more than 50 percent.

For Oregon and Washington, there is no going back. Washington will likely adopt all-mail voting in the near future because a majority of its population is voting absentee. And the requirements of the Help America Vote Act and other election laws that would apply to

counties operating polling places will likely seem especially burden-
some there, especially as the new machines and procedures would
only benefit a small sliver of the population.

All-mail voting systems have two great advantages over
traditional absentee ballots. First, the state mails ballots directly to
registered voters. There is no need for ballot requests and no intermediaries to request or deliver ballots. Second, all-mail systems are
essentially unitary systems.[2] All voting is done in the same way,
unlike every other kind of system, where a state must maintain
absentee and polling-place voting, and perhaps early voting as well.
The following recommendations apply to all-mail voting systems:

- While the direct mailing of ballots without request to
  all voters does reduce the opportunity for some forms
  of ballot-tampering and fraud, all-mail states still have
  the obligation to ensure that their ballots are as secure
  as possible. All-mail states rely almost exclusively on a
  signature check to determine the integrity of the ballot.
  These states should try to improve their signature-
  check systems as much as possible. While checking
  should proceed by hand, these states should also
  experiment with computer software to check signatures and flag those that do not match. Human checking is indispensable, but the checking of signatures by
  many different people in different locations under different conditions is bound to yield different standards.
  In addition, all-mail states have a special obligation to
  ensure there are no fraudulent voters registered on
  their lists and receiving absentee ballots.

- All-mail states should consider additional methods for
  identifying voters. While a check of voter identification at
  the polling place has become a controversial political
  issue, states with all-mail voting should consider some
  form of identification beyond the signature. Such states
  could require that every voter enclose a photocopy of
  some form of identification, not necessarily a photo ID.

- As all-mail states will necessarily separate the ballot from the privacy of a voting booth, the possibility of voter coercion is heightened. While detecting voter coercion is an extremely difficult task, all-mail voting states should make every effort to monitor such activities. They should publicize that it is a crime to coerce a vote. They should have easily available corruption hotlines for reporting abuses. They should hire independent investigators to survey voters about coercion and to uncover abuses. Even if such surveys find low levels of coercion, states should make them a regular part of their elections, so that if a concerted effort is made to coerce voters to affect an election, the state might detect it, prevent it, or pursue the perpetrators after the fact.

- All-mail states and private organizations in these states have an obligation to ensure that significant voter education events such as candidate debates occur early in the process, before ballots are mailed out and votes cast.

- Finally, if it turns out that a unitary system of all-mail voting is more cost-effective than a system of multiple voting methods, then all-mail states should not simply bank the savings, but should devote more resources to ballot security, increased voter registration outreach, and improved communication with voters.

The second category of high-absentee states consists of those in which less than half of the votes are cast by absentee. While there have been recent suggestions that Arizona and California move to all-mail voting, such a switch would be a major change from their current systems. Those states that have high-absentee voting should:

- Experiment with early polling-place voting. The political cultures of high-absentee states look favorably on "convenience" voting. But absentee voting is only one form of convenience. Early-voting states have also seen

great public support for their new systems. The introduction of early voting would provide competition for
absentee voting. It is not clear if people prefer to vote
at their kitchen tables, or if they merely prefer to vote
in advance of election day. Some high-absentee states
have significant numbers of people physically drop off
their ballots at clerks' offices or other central locations.
These voters might be equally willing to go to an early-
voting center and cast their ballots with the privacy
protections of the voting booth.

- Follow the recommendations for all-mail states by
  improving signature checks and experimenting with
  additional forms of identification for absentee voters.

- Make efforts to inform "permanent absentee voters" of
  the opportunities for election-day polling-place and
  early voting.

Recommendations for Early-Voting States. The group of states that has
moved toward early voting without greatly increasing absentee balloting is most in line with the general recommendations of this
report. Nonetheless, there are several aspects of early voting in
them that could be improved.

First, states should consider shortening the length of their
early-voting periods. Early-voting sites tend to be open two to
three weeks before election day. Shortening the period to a maxi-
mum of ten days, while increasing the number of voting hours
per day, could improve voter access, while avoiding problems that
arise when votes are cast far in advance of the election. With a
Tuesday election day, ten days before the election would cover
two weekends and the weekdays of the previous week. This
length of time should make the early-voting period convenient
for all but the few who are out of town on a long-term basis, or ill
or frail.

This shortened ten-day period may still be too long, as the critics
who promote a single election day would argue that a very concentrated

period of voting drives a civic pride and reminds people of the importance of voting. A diffuse election period could detract from interest
in voting. As a practical matter, however, most of the states with early
voting already have it for a period of two to three weeks prior to election day. It may be unrealistic for these states to go to a period of one
week or less. Scaling back to ten days, however, would not be such a
great change. Further, most candidate debates will likely have been
completed by this time, and early voters would see more of the political campaigns before they cast their votes. The period would also be
more concentrated and intense than it is today, which might promote
greater interest in the election.

With a shortening of the early-voting period should come a
lengthening of voting hours per day. Typically, early voting hours
parallel the workday, with 9 a.m. to 5 p.m. being common, or in
some cases 8 a.m. to 6 p.m. This is considerably shorter than most
states' election-day polling hours. If early voting is really meant to
be a convenience for voters, then it should take a cue from corpo-
rate America, where banks, doctors' offices, and other businesses
offer services in nonbusiness hours. I have recommended that
election-day voting be extended to 6 a.m. to 9 p.m., which is the
period of time several states already offer. It may not be practical for
early voting to follow those hours precisely, but it should be available to voters before and after work. Weekend hours for early voting vary widely, but in some places they are quite restrictive, and in
other places there are none. Given that the traditional workday
does not compete with voting on the weekend, it may not be necessary to have early morning or evening hours, but early voting
should be made available on both weekend days for substantial
hours. While increased hours at early-voting sites will surely cost
money, a reduced number of days might save money that could be
rededicated to providing longer hours.

A third step states could take to improve early voting would be
to offer it as close to election day as feasible. A number of states
have a long early-voting period, but it concludes the Friday before
the election. There are surely good reasons for such a break; in particular, states are right to ensure that the ballots at early-voting sites

are secured, machines safely moved to a new location, and other logistical and security measures are addressed before election day. States may have particular problems if their early-voting sites are different from their election-day sites. They may have to recalibrate and move machines and close down sites as well as open new ones. Despite these potential difficulties, states would do well to close the gap between the end of voting and election day. Ideally, they could have a compact and nearly seamless period of early voting that leads directly into election day. Arkansas, for example, has early voting on the Monday before the election.

Finally, states must strive to give voters the same protections at early-voting sites as at election-day polling locations. States where early voting has been introduced only recently have often had difficulty in their first election or two. Florida law, for example, did not treat early voting and election-day voting in the same way with respect to the zone near the polling location where votes may be solicited. There were complaints by voters that advocates for candidates could approach voters as they were very near the voting booth, which would not have been allowed on election day. States may wish to place early-voting centers in nontraditional locations such as malls, which might have constraints on how a polling place is set up. While some logistical compromises might be made, states should strive to make early voting and election-day voting as close as possible.

Recommendations for Mixed States. States with significant rates of absentee and early voting have made a commitment to convenience in voting.

The general recommendations of this study favor limited absentee voting and a short, concentrated period of early voting, along with a robust election day. Accordingly, mixed states should promote early voting and expand its hours and protections. States with a culture of voter convenience may not want to move back to old rules requiring voters to provide a reason for absentee voting, but they could make an effort to encourage would-be absentee voters to vote early if they cannot make it to an election-day polling place.

Similarly, those mixed states that offer permanent absentee status should limit it to those who have long-term commitments or conditions that prevent them from voting at an early or election-day polling place.

Clearly, these recommendations will be easier to follow for mixed states that have more early than absentee voting, but even those with significant absentee voting might find that they can shift a large fraction of those voters to early-voting locations.

Final Word

The United States is rapidly becoming a country that votes before election day. It is neither possible to ignore this trend, nor to put the genie back into the bottle. But we should worry about how these changes are affecting our elections. Absentee ballots are particularly worrisome because they remove the vote from the privacy protections of the polling place, may be cast far in advance of the election, and may dampen the enthusiasm and civic spirit that a very concentrated election period brings.

The answer is a rededication to making election-day voting better and the institution of a short, concentrated early-voting period. For those who need them, absentee ballots must always be available, but for the great majority of the electorate, there are other, better, convenient options that will focus attention and civic spirit on our elections.

Appendix I
Absentee and Early Voting, 2004

ABSENTEE AND EARLY VOTING, 2004

CATEGORY 1: LITTLE OR NO ABSENTEE OR EARLY VOTING

Name	2004 Estimated VAP (Voting Age Population)	Total Ballots Counted
Alabama	3,425,821	1,883,415
Connecticut	2,684,372	1,595,013
Delaware	629,009	377,407
District of Columbia	451,039	230,105
Illinois	9,518,482	5,361,048
Indiana	4,635,665	2,512,142
Kentucky	3,157,197	1,816,867
Louisiana	3,358,452	1,943,106
Maryland	4,200,854	2,395,127
Massachusetts	4,956,454	2,927,455
Minnesota	3,872,349	2,842,912
Mississippi	2,139,817	1,163,460
Missouri	4,344,660	2,765,960
Nebraska	1,316,475	792,910
New Hampshire	1,000,557	686,390
New Jersey	6,573,010	3,639,612
New York	14,790,540	7,448,266
Ohio	8,680,792	5,730,867
Oklahoma	2,664,520	1,474,304
Pennsylvania	9,615,172	5,769,590
Rhode Island	842,911	440,743
South Carolina	3,174,262	1,631,156
Utah	1,645,366	941,215
Virginia	5,695,220	3,223,156
Wisconsin	4,188,206	3,025,801
Total	**107,561,202**	**62,618,027**

Absentee Ballots Counted	Absentee Ballot Percent	Early Voting Ballots Counted	Early Voting Ballot Percent
63,266	3.4%	—	—
141,698	8.9%	—	—
18,360	4.9%	—	—
9,894	4.3%	—	—
191,177	3.6%	—	—
260,550	10.4%	—	—
98,661	5.4%	—	—
126,581	6.5%	—	—
139,440	5.8%	—	—
145,493	5.0%	—	—
231,711	8.2%	—	—
60,393	5.2%	—	—
204,607	7.4%	—	—
106,552	13.4%	—	—
62,059	9.0%	—	—
194,168	5.3%	—	—
337,544	4.5%	—	—
611,210	10.7%	—	—
64,076	4.3%	85,603	5.8%
282,710	4.9%	—	—
19,271	4.4%	—	—
157,990	9.7%	—	—
57,443	6.1%	—	—
221,890	6.9%	—	—
366,048	12.1%	—	—
4,172,792	6.7%	85,603	0.1%

(continued on next page)

(*continued from previous page*)

CATEGORY 2: HIGH ABSENTEE VOTING

Name	2004 Estimated VAP (Voting Age Population)	Total Ballots Counted
Alaska	470,027	314,502
Arizona	4,194,390	2,038,077
California	26,647,955	12,589,683
Iowa	2,274,174	1,497,741
Michigan	7,616,344	4,876,237
Montana	715,495	456,096
North Dakota	490,179	316,049
Oregon	2,766,936	1,851,671
Vermont	487,977	313,973
Washington	4,732,158	2,885,001
Wyoming	386,170	245,789
Total	**50,781,805**	**27,384,819**

CATEGORY 3: HIGH EARLY VOTING

Name	2004 Estimated VAP (Voting Age Population)	Total Ballots Counted
Arkansas	2,069,560	1,025,078
North Carolina	6,414,796	3,571,420
Tennessee	4,516,679	2,458,213
Texas	16,263,861	7,507,333
West Virginia	1,430,254	769,645
Total	**30,695,150**	**15,331,689**

Absentee Ballots Counted	Absentee Ballot Percent	Early Voting Ballots Counted	Early Voting Ballot Percent
62,017	19.7%	10,894	3.5%
830,874	40.8%	—	—
4,105,179	32.6%	—	—
460,059	30.7%	—	—
861,305	17.7%	—	—
91,076	20.0%	—	—
51,116	16.2%	6,523	2.1%
1,851,671	100.0%	—	—
60,072	19.1%	—	—
1,982,457	68.7%	—	—
47,008	19.1%	230	0.1%
10,402,834	**38.0%**	**17,647**	**0.1%**

Absentee Ballots Counted	Absentee Ballot Percent	Early Voting Ballots Counted	Early Voting Ballot Percent
41,432	4.0%	293,084	28.6%
122,984	3.4%	984,298	27.6%
57,676	2.3%	1,102,513	44.9%
283,159	3.8%	3,580,330	47.7%
20,004	2.6%	126,503	16.4%
525,255	**3.4%**	**6,086,728**	**39.7%**

(continued on next page)

(continued from previous page)

CATEGORY 4: MIX OF HIGH ABSENTEE AND EARLY VOTING

Name	2004 Estimated VAP (Voting Age Population)	Total Ballots Counted
Colorado	3,456,263	2,148,036
Florida	13,441,568	7,639,949
Georgia	6,534,852	3,317,336
Hawaii	980,154	431,203
Idaho	1,025,457	612,786
Kansas	2,049,512	1,199,590
Maine	1,037,050	754,777
Nevada	1,737,781	831,833
New Mexico	1,402,999	775,301
South Dakota	576,196	394,930
Total	32,241,832	18,105,741

Total for Categories 1–4	221,279,989	123,440,276

SOURCE: See Appendix 1 References.

Absentee Ballots Counted	Absentee Ballot Percent	Early Voting Ballots Counted	Early Voting Ballot Percent
600,075	27.9%	412,280	19.2%
1,336,297	17.5%	1,428,362	18.7%
282,857	8.5%	387,596	11.7%
83,098	19.3%	50,223	11.6%
34,609	5.6%	59,239	9.7%
134,361	11.2%	116,353	9.7%
80,761	10.7%	50,570	6.7%
93,364	11.2%	346,823	41.7%
156,020	20.1%	236,340	30.5%
35,912	9.1%	58,722	14.9%
2,837,354	15.7%	3,146,508	17.4%
17,938,235	14.5%	9,336,486	7.6%

Appendix I References

These references indicate the source for each state's data.

Alabama – According to the state Elections Department, there were 2,597,629 registered voters, 1,883,415 ballots counted, 63,266 absentee votes, and 1,899 provisional ballots counted in the 2004 general election.

Alaska – Data come from Kimball W. Brace and Michael P. McDonal, *Final Report of the 2004 Election Day Survey* (Washington, D.C.: Election Assistance Commission, 27 September 2005): 4–10.

Arizona – Data come from the *Final Report of the 2004 Election Day Survey.* In the survey, all voting before election day is classified as "Early Voting." The majority of people voting before election day vote by mail or they drop off completed ballots. I reclassified the data to reflect all voting prior to election day as "Absentee Voting."

Arkansas – According to the Secretary of State's office, there were 1,025,078 total ballots counted, 41,432 absentee votes counted, and 293,084 early votes counted.

California – According to the Secretary of State's website (http://www.ss.ca.gov/elections/sov/2004_general/contents.htm, last accessed on 21 August 2006), there were 12,589,683 total ballots counted and 4,105,179 absentee votes counted.

Colorado – Data come from the *Final Report of the 2004 Election Day Survey.*

Connecticut – Data come from the *Final Report of the 2004 Election Day Survey.*

Delaware – Data come from the *Final Report of the 2004 Election Day Survey.*

District of Columbia – Data come from the *Final Report of the 2004 Election Day Survey.*

Florida – Data come from the *Final Report of the 2004 Election Day Survey.*

Georgia – Data come from the *Final Report of the 2004 Election Day Survey.* In the survey data, Georgia reported 387,083 overvotes. I subtracted these overvotes from the reported absentee voting total of 669,940 to get 282,857 absentee votes.

Hawaii – Data come from the *Final Report of the 2004 Election Day Survey.*

Idaho – Data come from the *Final Report of the 2004 Election Day Survey.*

Illinois – Data come from the *Final Report of the 2004 Election Day Survey.*

Indiana – Data come from the *Final Report of the 2004 Election Day Survey.*

Iowa – The Secretary of State's *Report of Voters Registered and Voting* (http://www.sos.state.ia.us/elections/results/index.html, last accessed on 21 August 2006) reports 1,497,741 total ballots counted and 460,059 absentee votes counted.

Kansas – According to the Secretary of State's office, 250,714 ballots were cast before election day. According to *Voting and Registration in the Election of November 2004* (Washington, D.C.: U.S. Census Bureau, March 2006) 12 (http://www.census.gov/prod/2006pubs/p20-556 .pdf), 9.7% of voters participated in "Absentee Voting" and 8.4% participated in "Early Voting." Using this ratio, of the 250,714 votes cast prior to Election Day, I projected "Absentee Voting" and "Early Voting" at 134,361 ballots and 116,353 ballots, respectively.

Kentucky – Data come from the *Final Report of the 2004 Election Day Survey.*

Louisiana – According to the Secretary of State's office, there were 1,943,106 total ballots counted and 126,581 cast before election day. There is no reliable breakdown between "Absentee Voting" and "Early Voting," and Louisiana reported all of its ballots cast before election day as "Absentee Voting."

Maine – According to the *Final Report of the 2004 Election Day Survey*, 754,777 ballots were cast in the 2004 election. However, all breakdowns of the data are kept at the individual town level. Using percentages reported in *Voting and Registration in the Election of November 2004*, I projected "Absentee Voting" and "Early Voting" at 80,761 ballots and 50,570 ballots, respectively.

Maryland – Data come from the *Final Report of the 2004 Election Day Survey.*

Massachusetts – Data come from the *Final Report of the 2004 Election Day Survey*. However, only 280 of 351 jurisdictions reported source breakdowns. Such data are kept at the city level, making it impossible to compile better data.

Michigan – Data come from the *Final Report of the 2004 Election Day Survey.*

Minnesota – Data come from the *Final Report of the 2004 Election Day Survey.*

Mississippi – Data come from the *Final Report of the 2004 Election Day Survey*. However, no source breakdown was provided in the data. The Secretary of State's office reported 63,114 absentee votes less 2,721 that were discounted. Thus, 60,393 absentee ballots were counted. There is no early voting.

Missouri – Data come from the *Final Report of the 2004 Election Day Survey.*

Montana – Data come from the *Final Report of the 2004 Election Day Survey*. However, there were 76,234 overvotes reported in the data. Furthermore, the source data are broken down into 20% "Absentee Voting" and 11.6% "Early Voting." However, according to *Voting and Registration in the Election of November 2004*, it is clear that Montana does not have "Early Voting." I dropped the 11.6% "Early Voting" data because I believe that some jurisdictions reported absentee votes as both "Absentee Voting" and "Early Voting."

Nebraska – Data come from the *Final Report of the 2004 Election Day Survey*.

Nevada – Data come from the *Final Report of the 2004 Election Day Survey*.

New Hampshire – Data come from the *Final Report of the 2004 Election Day Survey*.

New Jersey – Data come from the *Final Report of the 2004 Election Day Survey*.

New Mexico – According to the Secretary of State's website (http://www.sos.state.nm.us/Main/Elections/2004/PDF's/Gensumm_04.pdf, last accessed on 21 August 2006), there were 775,301 total ballots counted, 156,020 absentee votes counted, and 236,340 early votes counted.

New York – According to the State Elections office, 337,544 absentee ballots were counted. These data include all 58 jurisdictions while only 53 were reported in the *Final Report of the 2004 Election Day Survey*.

North Carolina – Data come from the *Final Report of the 2004 Election Day Survey*.

North Dakota – Data come from the *Final Report of the 2004 Election Day Survey*.

Ohio – Data come from the *Final Report of the 2004 Election Day Survey*.

Oklahoma – Data come from the *Final Report of the 2004 Election DaySurvey*. However, there were 85,804 overvotes reported in the data. Furthermore, the source data is broken down into 10.2% "Absentee Voting" and 5.8% "Early Voting." However, according to *Voting and Registration in the Election of November 2004*, it is clear that the overvotes were double-counted as "Absentee Voting." I subtracted the overvotes from the "Absentee Voting" total to get the best number for "Absentee Voting": 64,076.

Oregon – Data come from the *Final Report of the 2004 Election Day Survey*. Oregon employs 100% vote-by-mail; thus I reclassified all data to reflect "Absentee Voting."

Pennsylvania – According to the Secretary of State's website, 5,769,590 ballots were counted in the 2004 general election, http://www.dos.state.pa.us/bcel/cwp/view.asp?a=1099. The data reported in the *Final Report of the 2004 Election Day Survey* did not include some of

Pennsylvania's largest jurisdictions. I took the 4.9% reported "Absentee Voting" and projected it for the entire state and came up with 282,710 absentee ballots.

Rhode Island – Data come from the *Final Report of the 2004 Election Day Survey*.

South Carolina – According to the Secretary of State's office, there were 1,631,156 total ballots counted and 157,990 absentee ballots counted.

South Dakota – According to the Secretary of State's website (http:// www.sdsos.gov/electionsvoteregistration/pastelections_electioninfo 04.shtm, last accessed on 21 August 2006), there were 94,634 total ballots cast before election day. All of these ballots were classified as "Absentee Voting," but South Dakota does have "Early Voting." Using percentages reported in *Voting and Registration in the Election of November 2004*, I projected "Absentee Voting" and "Early Voting" at 35,912 ballots and 58,722 ballots, respectively.

Tennessee – Data come from the *Final Report of the 2004 Election Day Survey*.

Texas – Data come from the *Final Report of the 2004 Election Day Survey*.

Utah – According to the Lieutenant Governor's office, there were 941,215 total ballots counted and 57,443 absentee votes counted.

Vermont – Data come from the *Final Report of the 2004 Election Day Survey*.

Virginia – Data come from the *Final Report of the 2004 Election Day Survey*.

Washington – Data come from the *Final Report of the 2004 Election Day Survey*.

West Virginia – Data come from the *Final Report of the 2004 Election Day Survey*.

Wisconsin – According to the Secretary of State's office, there were 3,025,801 total ballots counted and 366,048 absentee votes counted.

Wyoming – Data come from the *Final Report of the 2004 Election Day Survey*.

Appendix II

Voting Before Election Day
(percent of total vote)

VOTING BEFORE ELECTION DAY (PERCENT OF TOTAL VOTE)

State	1980	1982	1984	1986	1988	1990
AL	—	—	—	—	—	0.0
AK	—	—	—	—	—	—
AZ	—	—	—	—	—	—
AR	—	—	—	—	—	—
CA	6.2	6.5	9.3	9.0	14.1	18.4
CO	—	—	—	—	—	—
CT	—	—	—	—	—	—
DE	—	—	—	—	—	—
DC	—	—	—	—	—	—
FL	—	—	—	—	—	—
GA	—	—	—	—	—	—
HI	—	—	—	—	—	—
ID	—	—	—	—	—	—
IL	—	—	—	—	—	—
IN	—	—	—	—	—	5.7
IA	—	—	—	—	6.5	8.8
KS	—	—	—	—	—	—
KY	—	—	—	—	—	—
LA	—	—	—	—	—	—
ME	—	—	—	—	—	—
MD	—	—	—	—	4.2	2.7
MA	—	—	—	—	—	—
MI	—	—	—	—	—	—
MN	—	—	—	—	—	4.0
MS	—	—	—	—	—	—
MO	—	—	—	—	—	—
MT	—	—	—	—	—	—
NE	—	—	—	3.8	—	5.6
NV	—	—	—	—	—	21.3
NH	7.8	4.4	8.3	4.4	8.2	4.9
NJ	—	—	—	—	—	—
NM	—	—	—	—	—	—

1992	1994	1996	1998	2000	2002	2004
0.0	3.0	3.0	3.0	3.3	2.9	3.4
—	—	—	—	—	—	23.2
—	—	—	—	—	—	40.8
—	—	—	—	—	—	32.6
17.2	22.1	20.3	24.7	24.5	27.1	32.6
—	—	—	—	—	—	47.1
—	—	—	4.6	9.0	4.5	8.9
—	—	—	—	4.9	3.0	4.9
—	—	—	—	—	—	4.3
—	—	—	—	14.0*	—	36.2
—	—	—	—	—	—	20.2
10.6	14.3	15.3	17.1	19.7	28.6	30.9
—	4.1	9.1	9.6	10.9	10.5	15.3
—	—	—	—	—	—	3.6
7.0	6.6	7.4	6.9	8.5	7.5	10.4
10.2	12.7	15.9	15.3	21.2	23.7	30.7
—	—	14.0	11.2	17.0	16.4	20.9
—	—	—	—	4.4	3.7	5.4
3.2	3.6	3.6	1.8	4.7	2.7	6.5
—	—	—	—	—	—	17.4
4.6	3.1	3.9	3.2	4.7	3.8	5.8
—	—	—	—	—	—	5.0
—	—	—	—	—	—	17.7
5.7	4.8	5.6	4.4	6.7	4.9	8.2
—	—	—	—	—	—	5.2
—	—	—	—	—	—	7.4
—	—	—	—	15.0	—	20.0
—	5.0	6.0	5.0	11.5	8.7	13.4
25.6	25.0	22.7	18.4	29.3	30.8	52.9
8.4	4.9	7.4	4.9	7.8	—	9.0
—	—	—	—	—	—	5.3
—	—	—	—	31.0	44.2	50.6

(continued on next page)

(*continued from previous page*)

State	1980	1982	1984	1986	1988	1990
NY	—	—	—	—	—	—
NC	—	—	—	—	—	—
ND	—	—	6.1	2.2	7.6	—
OH	—	—	—	—	—	—
OK	2.6	0.7	3.0	1.9	3.0	1.9
OR	—	—	—	—	—	89.0
PA	—	—	—	—	—	—
RI	4.5	4.9	3.6	3.0	4.2	3.5
SC	—	—	—	—	—	—
SD	—	—	—	—	—	—
TN	—	—	—	—	—	—
TX	—	—	—	—	—	—
UT	—	—	—	—	—	—
VT	8.0	5.5	9.1	6.8	9.3	6.8
VA	—	—	—	—	4.9	2.1
WA	12.2	9.2	12.5	12.7	13.7	14.0
WV	—	—	—	—	—	—
WI	—	—	—	—	4.0	3.0
WY	—	—	—	—	—	—

*Only Early Voting

SOURCE: For 2004 data see Appendix I References. Data for the years prior to 2000 obtained from Secretaries of State's offices.

1992	1994	1996	1998	2000	2002	2004
2.5	1.9	2.5	1.3	2.7	1.1	4.5
—	—	—	—	2.5	—	31.0
7.9	6.2	6.6	8.4	12.9	14.7	18.3
—	—	—	—	—	—	10.7
6.5	4.1	5.0	3.7	6.3	5.2	10.1
90.2	88.3	48.0	100.0	100.0	100.0	100.0
—	—	—	—	—	—	4.9
4.1	3.6	4.0	3.0	4.0	3.1	4.4
—	—	—	—	6.9	6.6	9.7
—	—	—	—	—	—	24.0
—	17.7	22.7	21.8	38.0	35.9	47.2
—	—	—	—	39.0*	—	51.5
—	—	—	—	—	—	6.1
9.1	9.7	11.2	10.7	19.2	15.2	19.1
5.5	3.9	4.7	2.6	5.4	3.3	6.9
18.0	24.0	35.6	47.5	54.2	67.2	68.7
—	—	—	—	—	—	19.0
5.0	4.5	4.6	4.1	6.1	5.8	12.1
—	—	—	—	—	—	19.2

Notes

Introduction

1. See chapter 2 of this study.
2. See appendix I.

Chapter 1: A History of Absentee and Early Voting

1. Josiah Henry Benton, *Voting in the Field: A Forgotten Chapter of the Civil War* (Boston, 1915).

2. Ibid.; see also John Fortier and Norman Ornstein, "The Absentee Ballot and the Secret Ballot," *University of Michigan Journal of Law Reform* 36, no. 3 (Spring 2003): 496–500.

3. Benton, *Voting in the Field*; See also Fortier and Ornstein, "The Absentee Ballot and the Secret Ballot," 493, 496, 501.

4. George Frederick Miller, *Absentee Voters and Suffrage Laws* (Washington, D.C.: Daylion, 1948), 35.

5. Fortier and Ornstein, "The Absentee Ballot and the Secret Ballot," 488–92.

6. Ibid., 501–6.

7. Paul G. Steinbicker, "Absentee Voting in the United States," *American Political Science Review* 32 (October 1938): 898–90; P. Orman Ray, "Absent Voters," *American Political Science Review* 8, no. 3 (1914): 442–45; Fortier and Ornstein, "The Absentee Ballot and the Secret Ballot," 501–6.

8. Steinbicker, "Absentee Voting in the United States," 905.

9. Steinbicker, "Absentee Voting in the United States," 898–90; Ray, "Absent Voters," 442–45; Fortier and Ornstein, "The Absentee Ballot and the Secret Ballot," 501–6.

10. Miller, 19–20.

11. Special Committee on Service Voting, "Findings and Recommendations of the Special Committee on Service Voting," *American Political Science Review* 46, no. 2 (1952): 513.

12. Ibid., 521.

13. Pennsylvania Election Reform Task Force, "Military and Overseas Voting Historical Background and Statutory Requirements," March 2005, 2, http://www.dos.state.pa.us/election_reform/lib/election_reform/Military_and_Overseas_Voting_Historical_Background_and_Statutory_Requirements_Revised.pdf (accessed August 6, 2006).

14. Spencer D. Albright, "Election Legislation," *Book of the States* 14 (1962): 7.

15. Ibid., 20.

16. Ibid.

17. Robert Thornton, "Election Legislation," *Book of the States* 19 (1972): 26.

18. Ibid., 26.

19. Pennsylvania Election Reform Task Force, "Military and Overseas Voting," 2.

20. Ibid., 3.

21. California Secretary of State, "Historical Absentee Ballot Use in California," http://www.ss.ca.gov/elections/hist_absentee.htm (accessed August 14, 2006).

22. Samuel C. Patterson and Gregory Caldeira, "Mailing in the Vote: Correlates and Consequences of Absentee Voting," *American Journal of Political Science* 29, no. 4: 766–88; National Conference on State Legislatures, "Absentee and Early Voting," http://www.ncsl.org/programs/legman/elect/absentearly.htm (accessed August 6, 2006); Richard G. Smolka, "Election Legislation 1990–91," *Book of the States* 29 (1992): 261.

23. See appendix II.

24. Randy H. Hamilton, "American All-Mail Balloting: A Decade's Experience," *Public Administration Review* 48, no. 4 (September/October 1988): 860–66. For an early Nevada experiment with vote by mail for rural voters too far from polling places, see P. Orman Ray, "Absent-Voting Laws," *American Political Science Review* 18, no. 2 (May 1924): 321–25.

25. Richard G. Smolka, "Election Legislation," *Book of the States* 24 (1982): 91; Richard G. Smolka, "Election Legislation," *Book of the States* 25 (1984):181.

26. Smolka, "Election Legislation," *Book of the States* 25 (1984): 191. For a brief timeline of the history of Oregon's adoption of vote by mail, see Oregon Secretary of State, "A Brief History of Vote by Mail," http://www.sos.state.or.us/elections/vbm/history.html (accessed August 6, 2006).

27. Bill Bradbury (Oregon Secretary of State), Testimony for Election Administration Hearing , National Commission on Federal Election Reform, The Reagan Presidential Library, Simi Valley, California, April 12, 2001, available at http://www.sos.state.or.us/executive/speeches/041201.htm.

28. Richard G. Smolka, "Election Legislation," *Book of the States* 20 (1974): 206.

29. Field Poll, "Proportion of Voters Casting Mail Ballots Will Reach a New High in Today's Election," Release No. 2178, November 8, 2005, http://field .com/fieldpollonline/subscribers/RLS2178.pdf (accessed April 13, 2006).

30. O. Douglas Weeks, "Election Laws," *Handbook of Texas Online* http://www.tsha.utexas.edu/handbook/online/articles/EE/wde1.html (accessed August 6, 2006); Smolka, "Election Legislation," *Book of the States* 29 (1992): 261; "Citizens Enjoy Early Voting in Few States," *Michigan Daily Online*, October 21, 1996, http://www.pub.umich.edu/daily/1996/ oct/10-21-96/news/news4.html (accessed August 6, 2006).

31. See appendix I.

Chapter 2: The Extent of Absentee and Early Voting and Past and Future Trends

1. American National Election Studies, "The 2004 National Election Study [2004 ANES]," ftp://ftp.electionstudies.org/ftp/nes/studypages/2004 prepost/nes04var.txt (accessed August 15, 2006).

2. Annenberg Public Policy Center, University of Pennsylvania, "Early Voting Reaches Record Levels in 2004, National Annenberg Election Survey Shows," press release, March 25, 2005, http://www.annenbergpublicpolicy center.org/naes/2204_03_early%20votingpercent203_23_05_pr.pdf (accessed August 13, 2006).

3. U.S. Census Bureau, "Voting and Registration," *Current Population Surveys 1998–2006*, http://www.census.gov/population/www/socdemo/ voting.html (accessed August 15, 2006).

4. Ibid.

5. See appendix I.

6. U.S. Census Bureau, "Voting and Registration."

7. National Council of State Legislatures, "Absentee and Early Voting," October 27, 2004, http://www.ncsl.org/programs/legman/elect/absentearly .htm (accessed April 9, 2006).

8. See appendix II.

9. National Council of State Legislatures, "Absentee and Early Voting."

10. Ibid.

11. Michael W. Traugott and Michael Hamner, "Oregon Vote-by-Mail Project: Report to the League of Conservation Voters Education Fund" (University of Michigan, 2001), available online at http://www.lcveducation.org/ programs/polling-research/LCVEF_ORVote-By-MailResearch_02.doc.

12. Paul Gronke, "Early Voting Reforms and American Elections," paper presented at the 2004 annual meeting of the American Political Science

Association, Chicago, Ill., September 2–5, http://www.reed.edu/~gronkep/docs/Gronke-EarlyVoting-APSA2004.pdf (accessed April 9, 2006).

13. Robert Stein, Jan Leighley, and Chris Owens, "Electoral Reform, Party Mobilization and Voter Turnout," paper presented at the 2004 meeting of the Midwest Political Science Association, Chicago, Ill., April 21–23.

14. Benton, *Voting in the Field*, 311.

15. Steinbicker, "Absentee Voting in the United States," 898.

16. Special Committee on Service Voting, "Findings and Recommendations," 513.

17. William G. Andrews, "American Voting Participation," *Western Political Quarterly* 19, no. 4 (1966): 639–52.

18. American National Election Studies, "The 1968 National Election Study [1968 ANES]," ftp://ftp.electionstudies.org/ftp/nes/studypages/1968prepost/nes1968.txt (accessed August 15, 2006).

19. See appendix II.

20. U.S. Census Bureau, "Voting and Registration."

21. Patterson and Caldeira, "Mailing in the Vote."

22. See appendix II.

23. U.S. Census Bureau, "Voting and Registration."

24. "Questions Asked in NES Surveys," *American National Election Studies*, at http://www.umich.edu/~nes/resources/questions/questions.htm (accessed August 15, 2006).

25. U.S. Census Bureau, "Voting and Registration"; American National Election Studies, "The 1992 National Election Study [1992 ANES]" ftp://ftp.electionstudies.org/ftp/nes/studypages/1992prepost/nes1992.txt (accessed August 15, 2006); American National Election Studies, "The 2000 National Election Study [2000 ANES]" ftp://ftp.electionstudies.org/ftp/nes/studypages/2000prepost/anes_2000prepost_var.txt.

26. See appendix II.

27. American National Election Studies, "The 2000 National Election Study [2000 ANES]" ftp://ftp.electionstudies.org/ftp/nes/studypages/2000prepost/anes_2000prepost_var.txt (accessed August 15, 2006); American National Election Studies, "The 2004 National Election Study [2004 ANES]" ftp://ftp.electionstudies.org/ftp/nes/studypages/2004prepost/nes04var.txt (accessed August 15, 2006).

28. Gronke, "Early Voting Reforms," 5–6.

29. To reach these rough estimates, for 1996 and 2000 I used the rate of early voting in each state to determine the total number of early votes cast in Tennessee and Texas. I then used Census Bureau survey data to project a national total for 1996 and 2000, from which I could determine what

percentage Tennessee and Texas accounted for. For 2004, I used my adjusted EAC state and national numbers.

30. There are some states where small amounts of early voting have not increased dramatically. Oklahoma is an example. But states that emphasize early voting have been successful in promoting wide use of it quickly.

Chapter 3: Absentee and Early Voting: Voter Turnout and Voter Confidence

1. Bill Bradbury (Oregon secretary of state) and Sam Reed (Washington secretary of state), "The Voting Booth at the Kitchen Table," *New York Times*, August 21, 2001, available at http://www.sos.state.or.us/executive/ speeches/082101.html (accessed August 15, 2006).

2. Curtis Gans, "Making It Easier Doesn't Work; No Excuse Absentee and Early Voting Hurt Voter Turnout; Create Other Problems," Center for the Study of the American Electorate, report released September 13, 2004, 4, http://www.american.edu/ia/cfer/research/csae_09132004.pdf (accessed August 13, 2006).

3. Hamilton, "American All-Mail Balloting."

4. David B. Magleby, "Participation in Mail Ballot Elections," *Western Political Quarterly* 40, no. 1 (March 1987): 71–91.

5. Jeffrey A. Karp and Susan A. Banducci, "Going Postal: How All-Mail Elections Influence Turnout," *Political Behaviour* 22, no. 3 (2000): 223–39.

6. Priscilla Southwell and Justin Burchett, "The Effect of All Mail Elections on Voter Turnout," *American Politics Quarterly* 28, no. 1 (2000): 72–80; Michael W. Traugott, "Why Electoral Reform Has Failed: If You Build It, Will They Come?" in *Rethinking the Vote*, ed. Ann N. Crigler, Marion R. Just, and Edward J. McCaffery (New York: Oxford, 2004), 177.

7. Adam J. Berinsky, Nancy Burns, and Michael W. Traugott, "Who Votes by Mail? A Dynamic Model of the Individual-Level Consequences of Vote-by-Mail Systems," *Public Opinion Quarterly* 65 (2000): 178–97.

8. Gans, "Making It Easier," 2, 4

9. Berinsky et al., "Who Votes by Mail?" 194.

10. Karp and Banducci, "Going Postal: How All-Mail Elections Influence Turnout," 234.

11. Adam J. Berinksy, "The Perverse Consequences of Electoral Reform in the United States," *American Politics Research* 33, no. 4 (July 2005): 471–91.

12. J. Eric Oliver, "The Effects of Eligibility Restrictions and Party Activity on Absentee Voting," *American Journal of Political Science* 40, no. 2 (1996): 499–513.

13. Robert Stein with Jan Leighley and Chris Owens, "The Role of Candidates and Parties in Linking Electoral Reforms with Voter Participation," paper presented at the 2003 meeting of the Midwest Political Science Association, Chicago, Ill., April 21–23.

14. Patterson and Caldeira, "Mailing in the Vote."

15. Paul Gronke, Benjamin Bishin, Daniel Stevens, and Eva Galanes-Rosenbaum, "Early Voting in Florida, 2004," paper presented at the annual conference of the American Political Science Association, September 1, 2005, Washington, D.C., 13, http://www.reed.edu/~gronkep/docs/Gronke BishinStevensGalanes-Rosenbaum.APSA.2005.pdf (accessed April 9, 2006).

16. Magleby, "Participation"; Traugott, "Why Election Reform," 181.

17. Robert M. Stein and Patricia A. Garcia-Monet, "Voting Early But Not Often," *Social Science Quarterly* 78, no. 3 (1997): 665.

18. Lilliard E. Richardson Jr. and Grant W. Neeley, "Implementation of Early Voting: The Tennessee Elections of 1994," *Spectrum: The Journal of State Government* 69, no. 3 (Summer 1996): 16–23. Note that this was not a typical midterm election. Republicans took over both Houses of Congress, and Tennessee had two competitive Senate races on the same ballot.

19. James T. Smith and John Comer, "Consequential Reform or Innocuous Tinkering? Another Look at Efforts to Increase Turnout in American Elections," paper presented at the 2005 annual meeting of the Midwest Political Science Association, Chicago, Ill.

20. Gans, "Making It Easier," 3.

21. Gronke, "Early Voting Reforms."

22. Robert M. Stein, Jan Leighley, and Christopher Owens, "Who Votes, Who Doesn't, Why, and What Can Be Done?" Report to the Federal Commission on Electoral Reform, June 10, 2005, 11, http://www.american.edu/ia/cfer/0630test/stein.pdf (accessed August 21, 2006).

23. Bradbury and Reed, "The Voting Booth."

24. Priscilla L. Southwell and Justin Burchett, "Survey of Vote-by-Mail Senate Election in the State of Oregon," *PS: Political Science and Politics* 91, no. 2 (March 1997): 53–57.

25. Priscilla Southwell, "Five Years Later: A Re-Assessment of Oregon's Vote by Mail Electoral Process," *PS: Political Science and Politics* 98, no. 1 (2004): 89–93.

26. Bradbury and Reed, "The Voting Booth."

27. Gronke, "Early Voting Reforms," 4.

28. "Be Heard: National Poll," http://www.whytuesday.org/nationalpoll.html (accessed April 1, 2006).

29. Ibid.

30. See table 3-1. Note also that 7 percent or so said registration problems kept them from voting. While these results may point to an argument for greater convenience in registration, this study is more focused on convenience related to voting before election day.

31. James G. Gimpel, Ann Marie Leonetti, Joshua J. Dyck, and Daron R. Shaw, "Location, Knowledge and Time Pressures in the Spatial Structure of Convenience Voting," *Electoral Studies* 25, no. 1 (March 2006): 35–58.

Chapter 4: The Pitfalls of Absentee and Early Voting

1. Spencer Overton, "The Carter-Baker ID Card Proposal: Worse than Georgia," *Roll Call*, September 28, 2005.

2. John Fund, *Stealing Elections: How Voter Fraud Threatens Our Democracy* (San Francisco: Encounter Books, 2004), 145.

3. One exception to this rule is that a disabled voter may request assistance from another person in casting a ballot. But this exception proves the rule, because disability groups are among the strongest advocates for technology that allows all voters to cast votes themselves without assistance.

4. See chapter 1.

5. A longer account is available in Fortier and Ornstein, "The Absentee Ballot and the Secret Ballot," 496.

6. *Hartford Courant*, "Absentee Voting Corruption," June 11, 2004, A14.

7. Norm Maleng (King County prosecuting attorney), remarks at Double Voters Press Conference, Seattle, Washington, June 2, 2005, http://www.metrokc.gov/proatty/news/2005/repeatvotingtp.htm (accessed August 15, 2006).

8. Fund, *Stealing Elections*, 48–49.

9. Rex Bowman, "Town Officials in Wise County Indicted: Appalachia Mayor, 13 Others Charged with Fixing 2004 Election," *Richmond Times-Dispatch*, March 3, 2006.

10. Michael Moss, "Absentee Votes Worry Officials as Nov. 2 Nears," *New York Times*, September 13, 2004.

11. Oliver, "The Effects of Eligibility Restrictions," 499.

12. John McCormick and Jeff Zeleny, "Parties' Clarion Call; Vote Early, Vote Early," *Chicago Tribune*, September 22, 2004, C1.

13. Robert Tanner, "Call It Election Month: Growing Numbers of Early Voters Transforming Campaigns," Associated Press, September 11, 2004.

14. Ibid.

15. Ibid.

16. Moss, "Absentee Votes Worry Officials."

17. *In Re: The Matter of the Protest of Election Returns and Absentee Ballots in the November 4, 1997 Election For the City of Miami, Florida,* Case No. 98-507, District Court of Appeal of Florida, Third District.

18. John Mark Hansen quoted in Moss, "Absentee Votes Worry Officials."

19. There are some very slight exceptions to this rule. Oregon is also required to provide handicapped-accessible voting machines, but this affects an extremely small percentage of the vote.

20. Paul Gronke, "Ballot Integrity and Voting by Mail: The Oregon Experience." Report to the Commission on Federal Election Reform, Early Voting Information Center, Reed College, June 15, 2005, http://www.sos.state.or.us/executive/CarterBaker.pdf (accessed April 14, 2006).

21. Ibid.

22. Ibid.

23. Donald Green and Alan Gerber, *Get Out the Vote!: How to Increase Voter Turnout* (Washington, D.C.: Brookings, 2004), 34–41.

24. Ibid., 9

25. See chapter 2.

26. Ibid.

Conclusions and Recommendations

1. Robert Stein and Greg Vonnahme, "Election Day Vote Centers and Voter Turnout," paper presented at the 2006 annual meeting of the Midwest Political Science Association, Chicago, Ill. April 20–23, http://www.brookings.edu/gs/projects/electionreform/20060418Stein.pdf (accessed August 13, 2006).

2. Gronke, "Ballot Integrity and Voting by Mail."

About the Author

John C. Fortier is a research fellow at the American Enterprise Institute, where he serves as the principal contributor to the AEI-Brookings Election Reform Project. Fortier also writes a weekly column on Congress in *The Hill*, a Washington newspaper. Previously, while at AEI, he has served as executive director of the Continuity of Government Commission and project manager of the Transition to Governing Project. He recently edited and contributed to the third edition of *After the People Vote: A Guide to the Electoral College*.

He has taught political science at the University of Pennsylvania, the University of Delaware, Boston College, and Harvard University, and he has published articles in numerous political science and legal journals. He is a frequent radio and television commentator on the presidency, Congress, and elections.